MW01038730

WINGSHOOTING WISDOM
PRAIRIE

A Guidebook for Finding & Hunting Public Lands

BEN O. WILLIAMS

WILLOW CREEK PRESS

© 2006 Ben O. Williams

Cover painting and all interior paintings © Jim Borgreen
All black-and-white drawings are by the author.

Published by Willow Creek Press
P.O. Box 147, Minocqua, Wisconsin 54548

Library of Congress Cataloging-in-Publication Data
Williams, Ben O.
  Wingshooting wisdom. Prairie : a guidebook for finding and
hunting public lands / [Ben O. Williams].
      p. cm.
  ISBN 1-59543-425-9 (softcover : alk. paper)
 1. Upland game bird shooting--Great Plains--Guidebooks.
2. Public lands--Great Plains--Guidebooks. 3. Great Plains--
Guidebooks. I. Title.
  SK324.U6W55 2006
  799.2'460978--dc22

                                        2006010733

Printed in Italy

DEDICATION

*To everyone who shares wingshooting endeavors
in the prairie country I love.*

ACKNOWLEDGMENTS

I owe a special thanks to Darren Brown, Tom Carpenter, and Barbara Claiborn for their help, and to a host of friends and dogs who have hunted with me over the years.

CONTENTS

Key to Diet Icons

 Cultivated Head Crops: wheat, barley, corn, milo

 Cultivated Green Crops: seeds & greens, alfalfa, clover

 Grass & Sedge: greens & seeds, prairie, pasture, marsh, fescue, etc.

 Forbs: weeds, herbs, tubers, wood sorrels, etc.

 Fruits & Berries: woody plants, nuts, rosehips, strawberry, etc.

 Insects: grasshoppers, ants, beetles, etc.

 Animal matter: snails, frogs, mice, etc.

Key to Habitat Icons

 Grasslands: prairie, pasture, CRP (Conservation Reserve Program)

 Mountains: dense woody cover, shrubby understory, open parks

 Farmland: annual and perennial croplands

 Deserts: washes, arroyos, scrubland environment

 Riparian zones: woody areas along rivers and streams

 Savannas: mixed grass and trees

 Intermountain shrublands: woody brush mixed with grass, sagebrush

 Breaks: steep canyons, gullies, draws

 Forest: conifers, deciduous, cutover forest

 Wetlands: lowlands, marshes

 Homesteads: woodlots, abandoned farmsteads, windbreaks, etc.

 Open water: reservoirs, lakes, ponds

 Foothills: rolling country with draws

Why This Guide Book

The idea for developing a Wingshooting Wisdom guide series came to me on two fronts. After many years of hunting across North America, I realized that no helpful step-by-step guide existed for hunters interested in locating and hunting a single species of game bird. And as a photographer, author, and columnist for Pointing Dog Journal, I have received hundreds of inquiries over the years from traveling wingshooters who want to know how to zero in on birds in unfamiliar country.

This series is my response to those queries. Each guidebook will cover several species of game bird that live in close proximity or in similar habitat. The new and fresh ideas you'll learn will help you hunt more effectively whether you're a newcomer or veteran.

Part One of each guidebook will detail the best tactics for hunting each game bird. Part Two will show you methods for collecting valuable information on the best locations to hunt in a given year and area, and for gathering travel information.

Ben O. Williams
Livingston, Montana

FOREWORD

Long gone are the halcyon days when Robert Ruark's Old Man and the Boy could whistle an old bird dog from a shady spot under the porch and stroll to the open fields at the edge of town to put up covey after covey of birds. Times have changed. These days, it's all too easy to sit at home and grouse about shrinking access to private hunting land, hunting grounds lost to leasing, or public land overrun by other hunters or overgrazed by livestock. I used to do quite a bit of this myself to justify why I wasn't heading out to new areas as much as I used to. And it's true—access is shrinking, along with quality habitat in a lot of areas. But it's also an easy trap to fall into, because it's not the whole truth.

The rest of the story is outlined in this series of unconventional guidebooks that not only help you better understand game birds and how they utilize their environment, but also teach you a proven method for locating those elusive birds on hunting trips far from home, where you don't have the luxury of unlimited scouting time. You may find it hard to believe, but the average hunter still can find quality hunting for various game birds across the country, both on public and private land. The proof is in these pages.

Ben Williams has been chasing prairie birds for a very long time and can do so fairly close to home, but he still hits the road each year in search of new hunting country. And he finds it. These places tend to be far from population centers, far from areas that casual hunters with just a few hours to hunt can reach. Many are on public lands or private lands open to hunting through state-run programs, places available to anyone willing to do some homework.

Thomas Edison once said that many people don't recognize opportunity because it's dressed in overalls and looks like hard work. And I think that's the case for a lot of wingshooters today. Finding untrammeled hunting grounds can be difficult, so hunters tend to stay home or find something else to do after the opening weekend of bird season. But it doesn't have to be that way. The method Ben has developed for locating excellent hunting opportunities when local bird populations are at their peak was honed through many years of experience. If you follow this plan closely you will soon be able to zero in on your own new hunting areas, all without killing yourself in the effort or spending huge sums of money.

Hunting trips for the traveling wingshooter should be more than just driving aimlessly down back roads for hours while the dogs whine in the back of the truck and you become increasingly frustrated. Read this book and you'll soon know everything you need to know to make your next trip the best you've ever had, and you'll pick up a wealth of hunting and traveling tips, as well.

—Darren Brown
Editor, *For the Love of a Dog*

SHARP-TAILED GROUSE
Tympanuchus phasianellus

Size and Weight
length: 16-18"
weight: 1.5-2.5 pounds

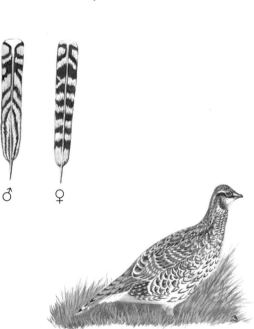

♂   ♀

PART ONE

SHARP-TAILED GROUSE

A Plentiful Bird on the Great Plains

East of the Rocky Mountains the lands sweeps down across a huge prairie known as the Great Plains. Vast herds of bison once migrated across the plains, feeding on the lush, abundant grasses. Nomadic Indian tribes followed these animals, thriving on the bounty of the land.

Next, explorers, trappers, and horse solders visited the grasslands; roadside monuments still commemorate their names today. Then came the cattle barons and sodbusters, who permanently changed the face of the landscape. In the early 1900s, millions of acres of native grassland came under the plow, and domestic crops soon covered much of the prairie.

Waves of European immigrants settled in the Dakotas and other prairie states, using the Homestead Entry Act to acquire the land and grow crops on their claims. Farm commodity prices had increased substantially during and after World War I, and at first the highly erodible soil was very productive. Rainfall was abundant and the land yielded adequate crops for many seasons. Inspired by these two factors, homesteaders cultivated over twenty million acres of the Great Plains by 1928. However, the settlers' good fortune ended when commodity prices fell

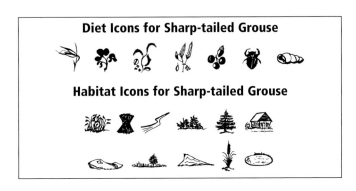

Diet Icons for Sharp-tailed Grouse

Habitat Icons for Sharp-tailed Grouse

at about the same time that the great drought of the mid-1930s began.

Land that should never have been turned over by the plow lost its topsoil, which was swept away by dry, scouring winds. Clouds of fine, dusty soil rolled across miles of misused grasslands, making roads impassable and burying fence lines and farmsteads. The dreams of thousands of homesteaders blew away with that topsoil. The Dust Bowl brought disaster to rural areas, and the Great Depression only made things worse. To save the land, the federal government purchased many ruined homesteads from hopeless landowners, and the national grasslands were born.

Today these grasslands are managed by the Department of Agriculture, U.S. Forest Service. Under the multiple-use concept, the national grasslands offer a wide range of recreational opportunities, including bird hunting. Many of these areas have been restored over the years, and prime prairie grouse habitat is once again available. There are currently twenty national grasslands totaling nearly four million acres—nearly all of it available to hunters.

For more information, contact the district ranger at the location you plan to hunt.

Call 'Em What You Like

In the past, both pinnated grouse (prairie chickens) and sharp-tailed grouse were abundant in the Plains States, although homesteaders usually classified all prairie game birds as "wild chickens." Even today, a few long-time rural residents still lump all grouse together under this heading, although most folks in the region now refer to them simply as chickens and grouse, respectively. For bird hunters, it's more common to call them sharptails and prairie chickens.

In Flight and in the Hand

Not many of North American game birds are easily identified in flight. This is especially true when a bird flushes some distance away and under low-light conditions. But with a little study, the hunter can learn to recognize each bird's flight pattern. Color alone is not the best way to identify a bird on the wing. Observing its color, size, shape, movement, wing beats, sounds, and the habitat from which it was flushed all play a role in quick identification.

Experienced hunters immediately recognize sharptails in flight by their plump bodies, short pointed tails, and the predominant whiteness of their underbodies. Their short wings beat rapidly for a few seconds, and then stop as they

Distribution Map: The red line indicates historical range. There are many gaps within present range due to loss of habitat and human activity.

glide for a distance and repeat the pattern over and over again. Sharptails often make a low-pitched kuk-kuk-kuk-kuk several times after being flushed. But at times this soft call is barely audible. Both sexes look the same in flight.

No other game bird shares the same characteristics, along with the habitat, of the sharptail. The one exception could be a young hen pheasant, which during the early weeks of grouse season appears similar, although pheasants have an elongated shape and a longer tail.

In the hand, a sharptail is easy to identify. The general coloration of the two sexes is almost identical—light brown, with markings of black, buff, white. The head is buff colored. Look for a pattern of brown V-shaped breast markings set off in white. The tail is relatively short, rarely exceeding six inches. Sex can be determined by examining the two longer feathers in the center of the tail. The female has cross-barring on these feathers, while the male has more linear dark lines with no cross bars. Adult males also exhibit yellow eye combs and small bare skin neck sacs.

A sharptail is larger than a ruffed grouse and a bit smaller than a prairie chicken. Average weight is less than two pounds. Males are a bit larger than females, but that's difficult to determine in the field.

Sharp-tailed grouse once occupied suitable habitat across a huge swap of North America. Several subspecies inhabited different kinds of country. At one time, these different races occupied the scrub forests, grasslands, steppes, savannas, and agricultural lands of the Midwest and western plains. Their range covered parts of twelve states and six Canadian provinces, including the Yukon and Northwest Territories.

Two races of sharp-tailed grouse have suffered considerably from habitat changes in their historical range. One of these is the Columbian sharp-tailed grouse, which lost most of its wide distribution. The other is the prairie race of sharp-tailed grouse, which has been extirpated in much of its range.

In the central Plains States and Canadian provinces, the plains sharp-tailed grouse and greater prairie chicken are faring well, but even there much work needs to be done to secure suitable habitat.

Today, the plains sharp-tailed grouse is the most important subspecies when it comes to hunting. It's a resident of portions of Alberta, Saskatchewan, Montana, Wyoming, North and South Dakota, Nebraska, Colorado, and even parts of Kansas and Oklahoma. The northern race of sharptail is also an important game bird throughout much of its range. The general characteristics of each race of sharp-tailed grouse differ a little, but their basic requirements are similar. Even though this chapter focuses primarily on the plains sharp-tailed grouse, the information here also applies to the other huntable subspecies.

A Bit of History

There is evidence that the early trappers of the Hudson Bay Company were the first white people to encounter the prairie sharp-tailed grouse. They explored far into the interior in the north-central states and central Canada, where they soon learned that the sharptail was not a game bird of continuous mature forests, but of forest openings. A bird of succession and brushlands.

The fact that the sharp-tailed grouse formerly lived over a vast area of North America is proof that much of the northern forests once had large open areas, often in the form of bogs and marshlands that kept the normally dense woods free of woody growth. Huge fires within the mature forest, clearing a natural climax succession of low cover, caused other large openings.

Once settlers migrated westward, great changes occurred in the landscape. This had a monumental effect on the habitat. Homesteaders cleared much of the brushy land, removing good sharptail cover, although their close cousin the prairie chicken quickly moved in. By then, loggers were clearing vast areas of old-growth forest, and forest fires continued to add new areas of excellent cover. Sharptails expanded into this open brushy range.

Once a species moves into new surroundings, the birds tend to overpopulate it before dropping back to a normal

Male sharp-tailed grouse dancing on lek (breeding grounds).

carrying capacity. Once called "fire grouse" because they thrived after a big burn, large flocks of sharptails furnished considerable food for homesteaders, lumber camps, and boomtowns.

This period of cutover forests and huge fires was fairly short-lived. Most of the open areas soon grew back or were reforested, becoming too thick for sharptails. Many farms were abandoned and eventually returned to mature forest, also adding to the demise of brushland open habitat. These changes eventually reached a stage where most of the bird's habitat was gone.

The cumulative effect of these habitat losses has been so

great that the future of the prairie sharptail is not as bright as it should be. Thanks to dedicated wildlife biologists, state and federal wildlife agencies, the North American Grouse Partnership, and other helpful organizations, sharptails are slowly recovering portions of their historic range. The fate of the prairie sharp-tailed grouse is in our hands, we'll have no one to blame but ourselves if quality habitat isn't preserved.

Behavior

Whether you are a veteran or novice hunter, knowing the habits and habitat of a species is an essential part of becoming a more savvy and observant wingshooter. Learning a new game bird's social behavior is always time well spent. This information will help you know what to look for in the field and give you the pleasure that comes with completely understanding your quarry.

Sharp-tailed grouse requirements for food, moisture, dusting, roosting, lofting, and social interaction vary from day to day and through each season of the year. Like all game birds, sharptails have three different yearly activities: breeding and female nesting from March to June; females raising their broods into adulthood and staying in small family groups during June to September; and both sexes forming small social groups and sorting into large winter flocks from September to March. After the breeding season, adult males have no further involvement with the rearing of young. They become more solitary until all the birds gather into winter flocks.

If you have a chance, it's a good idea to visit a sharp-tailed grouse breeding ground in the spring. This gathering place is called a "lek." The mating ritual is a unique event and enjoyable to observe. Groups of male grouse gather, then dance and fight to attract hens. Some leks are traditional, seeing activity year after year, but most are used only for a few seasons because of physical changes to the land.

Depending on winter carryover and population going into the breeding season, the number of adults visiting a lek fluctuates from year to year. Data collected from spring counts are very helpful to biologists in projecting the outlook for fall hunting numbers.

By late April to mid-May the hen has chosen a nesting place on the ground, usually less than a mile from the dancing grounds. The specific timing for nesting and hatching changes according to latitude and prevailing weather conditions. The nest is well hidden, generally in brushland cover with open areas close by. Clutch size can be from six to sixteen, but the average is around ten.

If the hen happens to lose her nest early in incubation, she will probably nest again. Sharptails do not bring off more than one brood each year, though. If you see a late brood, it's usually from a female that has been forced to renest.

Incubation takes about twenty-one days, and the brood is led away from the nest after the last egg has hatched. The first few weeks after hatching are a critical time for the chicks. They are vulnerable to predation at this time, but weather plays a much bigger role in chick survival. Wet, cold conditions are the real culprit. The weather itself does-n't often directly affect the chicks, but the results of that weather usually impact the available food supply. The chicks' main food is insects, and nasty weather slows down the development of most bugs. Without insects, chicks don't get enough protein to produce thermo energy or rapid grown during this critical period, which leads to a higher mortality rate.

The territory of the new brood is fairly limited; they travel less than a quarter-mile per day. When protein sources are abundant the chicks grow very rapidly. And within ten to twelve days the little birds can fly a short distance. At four to five weeks they start feathering out and can fly quite well. Once the young birds reach twelve weeks old they are fully feathered and look similar to the mother. They become strong fliers, but still prefer to walk when possible. If flushed, they rarely fly very far.

Their behavior at this stage is much like an adult's, and they become somewhat independent. The young birds begin to spread out when dusting or loafing and will travel some distance from the mother when foraging for food. But the young birds still gather together in a loose cluster on the ground to roost.

Late summer is a real turning point in the behavior of young adults. The juveniles continue to feed on insects when available, but also forage on summer fruits and greens. By late September the young birds are physically adults. They have little reason to travel far at this time of year, as food is abundant. If cereal grains are present nearby, they will start using the cut fields to feed.

As late fall approaches, the family unit begins to break up and small groups band together. Flock sizes increase, but these are loose groups that often disband if the weather turns warm. The birds typically get back together again after a change of weather.

Handsome full-grown sharptail.

Winter changes the sharptail's movements. Food becomes harder to find, so the birds must travel greater distances each day to find feeding and roosting areas. Larger flocks band together and feed on fruits and weed seeds found in brushland habitat. When winter snows arrive, grouse turn to buds and hanging fruit for sustenance and spend most of their time in a brushland environment. By mid-winter, the large groups begin to break up again. And as spring draws near, the birds look to their dancing ground, repeating the cycle.

Living Requirements

Sharp-tailed grouse are the most plentiful native game bird of the Great Plains. But the traveling wingshooter still needs to recognize good sharptail habitat to have success. There is no doubt that much of the bird's range has been lost due to human development over the years. Intensive grazing and clean farming have removed thousands of acres of good habitat, but plenty of huntable land remains.

The nucleus of sharp-tailed grouse habitat is brushy cover. Brushland cover is to sharptails what sage is to sage grouse and grasslands are to prairie chickens. The key to good sharptail habitat is brushy cover mixed with grasslands or croplands, and it makes little difference what kind of woody cover there is as long as there is plenty of it. In some regions, there is relatively little tree cover, so sharptails become more dependent on low shrubby cover for food and protection. If adequate brushland and grassland are maintained, sharptails will eventually find it.

The general rule for ideal sharptail habitat is at least 10- to 40-percent woody cover, preferably in clumps rather than scattered as in a savanna.

Sharptails can adapt somewhat to modern agriculture and cattle ranching, as long as the woody cover has not been eliminated and some standing grasses are still available. Sharptails need fall carryover grassy cover in the winter and spring for shelter, protection from predators, roosting, and nesting. Woody cover in the form of trees or brushy shrubs is essential for winter survival, food, rest, and escape.

Knowing what a bird eats is essential for knowing where and how to hunt that species. Sharptails are no exception, despite the fact that they consume a greater variety of foods

Sharp-tail Grouse Ground Sign

The knowledge of signs on the ground left by a sharp-tail grouse is very helpful in knowing that they are using an area to feed, roost, or loaf, and can save time in the field when looking for that species.

Tracks: look for tracks in sand, snow and mud

Single droppings: look for single droppings in open grasslands and open cut crop fields.

Roosting site droppings: birds roost singly, but family flocks use the same areas.

Feathers: single feathers can be found in feeding and dusting areas.

than other game birds. Their diet changes as the hunting season progresses, and smart hunters adapt their tactics accordingly. As mentioned above, young sharptails mostly eat insects. But as they mature, greens are added to the menu. Both adults and juveniles will continue to eat insects as long as they are available, but the daily diet shifts primarily to vegetable matter. Over 90 percent of their yearly diet comes in the form of greens, seeds, fruits, and grains. In late summer and early fall, foods include large amounts of lush grasses, clover, alfalfa, dandelions, and succulent fruits.

As the season progresses, greens are still consumed when available, but rose hips, snowberries, chokecherries, hawthorn, and many other varieties of wild fruit are eaten in large numbers. Dry seeds are also important in the fall, and if croplands are within the birds' range, grains are consumed whenever available.

With the onset of winter, sharptails continue to feed on whatever fall food isn't covered with heavy snow. Dried fruits, waste grain, mast, and seeds are all consumed as long as possible. But winter brings a great change in the sharptails' diet. They turn to tree buds, twigs, catkins, mast, and the many low shrubs remaining above the snowline. In the leanest months, they will eat just about any kind of vegetable matter available.

No matter what time of the season you hunt sharptails, get in the habit of taking a crop sample from any birds you shoot to see what kinds of food they are eating. This information will help you locate other birds, which will likely be utilizing similar food sources.

Hunting Strategies

Sharptails typically inhabit wild country, and not many hunters are willing to explore it. When going after sharptails for the first time it's essential to learn as much as possible about their movements, locations during the day, and feeding habits. By preparing yourself before your trip, you will save valuable time in the field—and that's always critical for the traveling wingshooter.

Sharp-tail Grouse and the
Conservation Reserve Program

Many state and federal agencies have restored public lands for the benefit of wildlife. For over a decade, the federal government has implemented the Conservation Reserve Program (CRP), a national conservation program that provides incentives to landowners that take marginal soils out of production. These lands are then seeded to create grasslands and brushy cover. Over the years, this program has been a boon to all wildlife and has restored thousands of acres of suitable habitat for sharp-tailed grouse.

Each year I try to hunt a different location for prairie game birds. I enjoy being in new country and studying the lay of the land, the habitat, and how to find birds. I do my homework beforehand and make sure the information I receive about the best time to go is correct. This is vital to finding birds. My advice to anyone planning to hunt an unfamiliar area for new species is to first take into account the ideal time to hunt that area.

The prairie game bird season begins in September across most of the northern Plains States, starting with Montana's opener on September 1. The ideal time for hunting sharptails is typically from opening day to mid-October. Daytime temperatures can occasionally get warm at this time, but the nights are chilly, and morning frost usually touches the prairie.

The birds are still in their loose family groups during this period, and they are feeding primarily on the fall crop

The edges of sagebrush country can be outstanding for hunting sharptail.

of grasshoppers and new ripe berries. Food is abundant for game birds in September, and as the insect population starts to diminish the sharptails focus on picking berries and gleaning cereal grains. But remember, sharptails are primarily a bird of open country or brushland, so they prefer to feed in areas of tall grassy cover or in brushy draws and coulees.

Weather also influences the type of cover being used, daily feeding times, and the kind of food consumed. On bright, warm days, the birds will fly to feeding grounds early in the morning and return to shady spots at midday to take life easy. Early morning is about the only time you can find them in short, green cover or cutover cropfields. Sharptail feeding activities change in cold or stormy conditions. They may not leave their roost sites until late morning. As the days become shorter, sharptails spend more time feeding on grain and weed seeds.

Sharptail range is large compared to many other upland game birds, and they feed on a wide variety of food. So as the season progresses, it's important to be aware of the habitat and the kinds of food available when you arrive in new territory. The terrain has to fit the daily needs of the birds. I usually seek out the highest ground first so I can view the whole terrain and identify the most likely sharptail hangouts before hunting in earnest.

I pursue sharptails throughout the long hunting season where I live, but I wouldn't recommend that traveling hunters plan trips after mid-October. In many parts of the Great Plains the weather is unpredictable, and by this time the birds start to flock and often become more difficult to approach. Also, in many areas, sharptails and pheasants occupy the same country and their hunting seasons overlap. Pheasants are America's number-one game bird, so more folks will be in the field at this time. And once the pheasant season starts many landowners close their lands to other types of hunting due to commitments to family and friends.

But if you do your sharptail hunting before the pheasant crowd goes afield you just may have the best hunting grounds to yourself. And, for me, that's what bird hunting is all about.

The time of day is important in relation to the kind of

cover in which the birds are feeding, resting, and loafing. Be aware of the daily weather forecast and the long-term weather pattern for the area you're hunting. Look for bird sign such as feathers, droppings, and dusting places. Then determine how fresh they are.

Once you find sharptails and all the excitement of the flush is over, evaluate what they were doing and what type of habitat they were utilizing. Mark the rest of the birds down, or at least remember the direction they were traveling. If a late bird gets up, make a mental note of where it goes. Many times, the last bird will take a shortcut that reveals exactly where the other birds went. Not only do you have a good chance of finding them again, but you may find a new bird hangout you were unaware of, which can be

Darren Brown hunting the high plains with his two fine German shorthaired pointers.

helpful for future hunts. And don't forget to examine the crops of any birds you shoot. The more you know about what birds are eating and where they are eating it, the more successful your hunts will be.

About Dogs

Many experienced bird hunters use flushing dogs to hunt sharptails. These dogs are usually at their best in heavy cover, so the most effective method is to work the draws and coulees and go through heavy patches of cover strung along the way. These close-working dogs plow through the brushy cover and force the birds into the air. This works great, but flushing dogs are not used much in big open grassy country. Not because they can't find birds there, but because grass-lands often seem so overwhelmingly vast.

I believe prairie game birds were made for pointing dogs, although sharptails demand the best from high-quality dogs. Many bird hunters don't believe an adult sharptail will hold for a pointing dog, and I readily admit that this is true in certain situations.

Young sharptails, or ones not hunted often, behave very well for pointing dogs. But an inexperienced pointing dog first has to learn the ways of these birds. A pointer that has been trained on pen-raised planted birds will not do well on sharptails right out of the dog crate, neither will dogs used to wild, running pheasants. A pointing dog that hunts wild pheasants often has trouble with moving sharptails. The dog just gets too close. It takes a smart pointing dog—

whatever the breed—to learn to be more cautious and not crowd sharptails.

Sharptails may well be one of the hardest game birds for a young pointer to adjust to hunting. A pointing dog must approach every species of game bird differently. Sharptails are flock birds, but they usually spread out while feeding or resting, so dogs are generally pointing only one or two birds instead of the whole group. Also, as the season progresses, it becomes more difficult for a dog to hold the birds. He has to learn to point them from farther away. And a mature flock of sharptails can't be hunted day after day and still be expected to hold well. Sharptails become very wary when pushed often, just like other wild game birds.

Over the years, I have observed several other important reasons why sharptails give inexperience dogs a fit. A single sharptail doesn't lay down a lot of scent compared to other birds, particularly in heavy cover, where its scent may be overwhelmed by the surrounding vegetation. If cover is sparse, sharptails will move slowly away from any intruder instead of sitting still. So dogs have to learn not to push the birds.

Hunters whose dogs are new to sharptails need to be patient and give the dogs time to figure things out.

Where to Go

The outlook for this wonderful prairie bird's next few years is promising. CRP is expanding in the Great Plains. North and South Dakota, Nebraska, Wyoming, Montana, Alberta, and Saskatchewan have had good populations of sharptail for the past several seasons. If the spring weather patterns stay about the same, the future for hunting in these states and provinces looks good.

They Weren't Where They Were Supposed to Be

The stubble was cut higher than usual. I put beeper collars on Mac and Pat, my two older Brittanys, and started down the long golden wheatfield. The sky was a pale blue, with not a

Hunting sharptails in CRP; Brittany holding a large male.

cloud in sight. I figured that by noon the temperature would be in the high seventies. When I got to the end of the long strip it was already hot, so I called the dogs in for water. We then crossed a low wire fence and a two-rut road, skirting a broken-down wooden fence to check out an alfalfa field before heading back toward the hunting rig.

The green field was cool, releasing the morning dew. The second-growth alfalfa was thin and had not been cut. Both dogs moved freely in the sparse cover, their heads held high to scent the air. Far ahead, the dogs disappeared, dropping out of sight over a low swale. I quickened my pace when I heard the beepers go silent for a moment, and then change modes to the hawk scream.

"Dogs on point," I said to myself.

After I walked by both Brittanys, the dogs relocated and stopped again. I looked for movement beneath the pale blue flowers, gun held ready, waiting for a rush of wings to grab air. The dogs moved in, but nothing happened. I turned around to look back just as a lone rooster pheasant flushed and thundered past me. But no sharptails. The evidence was clear, though; each time the dogs got birdy and stopped momentarily, I found fresh sharptail droppings nearby. We crisscrossed the field several times, but the sharptails just weren't where they were supposed to be. Why the birds had used the field yesterday but not today puzzled me.

Not having found a single bird, I returned to the pickup for lunch. I gave the dogs a drink of water and they lay under the tailgate while I ate a sandwich and thought about going someplace else. Glancing up at the sky, it occurred to me that yesterday's weather was rainy and overcast. I reasoned that the droppings I'd seen were from birds feeding in the hay meadow at midday. But with today's clear weather the birds had probably fed earlier in the morning, and I'd missed them.

After lunch the dogs worked across a stubble field that ran along the edge of the sagebrush flat before I called them back. I didn't want them to work the big coulee that runs through the sage without my being close. Sagebrush is good lofting cover, but I was sure the birds would be on the side hill of the deep coulee, under a canopy of buffalo berries.

The Brittanys made a long cast far to my right, and I

lost sight of them in the tall, heavy sagebrush. Aromatic sage filled my nostrils, and I knew that with the strong scent and hot afternoon it would be tough for the dogs to pick up bird scent. Then I heard the beepers sound the hawk scream. One dog came into view as I walked through the sage, and I heard the other beeper sound off far ahead. I walked past the first dog, and moved slowly alongside the lead dog. With a clap of wings, several waves of young sharptails lifted skyward.

I put the two dogs in their compartment before I dressed out the brace of sharptails I'd taken. An examination of the contents of the birds' crops showed that they had indeed been feeding on waste grain in the wheatfield that morning. But I never imagined the sharptails would be hanging out in the sagebrush.

GRAY PARTRIDGE
Perdix perdix

Size and Weight
length: 13″
weight: .5 to 1 pound

♂   ♀

GRAY PARTRIDGE

The Waterfall Covey

On the Great Plains, there seems to be no limit to how far you can walk under the boundless sky or how much your eyes can see from horizon to horizon. More days than I can remember, I have drifted for hours with hard-running dogs over miles of hills, draws, and flats in pursuit of gray partridge. The hunting rig is often reduced to a tiny silhouette in the distance. Watching a breeze run through the mixed grasses beneath my feet makes me feel insignificant in the open world of the prairie. The expansive surroundings expose me to the elements, yet also reveal the places I love to hunt in the sea of grass.

In September, early frost initiates the dying phase of most prairie plants. Forbs display their variety of colors and the herbaceous shrubs become leaden with bright berries. The migrating birds and other creatures of the prairie change their routine to prepare for the coming winter.

It's been warm for the past week, but on this day, winter seems all too close. Low clouds hang over the horizon and cover the sun. A northern breeze carries much needed cool moisture and fills the air with aromatic signs of autumn.

I park the hunting rig next to a small earthen dam. A family of blue-winged teal moves to the other end of the

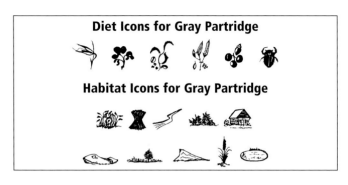

Diet Icons for Gray Partridge

Habitat Icons for Gray Partridge

pothole when I release young Winston, Pat, and Perk. As the three dogs approach the water's edge, a flock of tricolor blackbirds stage momentarily on a cluster of cattails, then break the silence with a whirl of wings and vanish.

The high golden grass buckles underfoot, slowly stretching skyward again after each step. Watching the dogs run at top speed, I'm thinking this should be a good day for scenting; the wind is moist and most of the green vegetation is gone. The climb is steep, so I stop to catch my breath at the top of the ridge. I know this country, and every landmark is anchored in my mind. Below me, there's a grassy slope that feeds precious water down to a brushy, cottonwood-lined drainage during spring runoff. Far below to my right the creek abruptly descends over a rocky sandstone wall. Some years the dogs drink from the waterfall, but today the falls are dry, so there's no need to stop.

I know the whereabouts of two coveys of Huns that feed along the slope. I can't see them, but they are there, nonetheless.

Down the grassy slope we go. I try not to move too fast or lose sight of the dogs. Halfway down, the earth folds and a small rise obscures my view of the dogs and the creekbed. Minutes later I hear the beepers sounding the pointing mode. Silently, I move up the incline.

The sounds of the beepers resonate for some time before I reach the top of the hill. Young Winston is steadfast at the bottom of the grassy draw that feeds into the dry wash. The other two dogs are strung out steady as rocks. I carefully move past Pat and Perk. Winston is facing me at the far edge of a large patch of buck brush. The birds appear to be between Winston and me. Side-by-side ready, I square my shoulders and walk toward him.

Gun, dogs, and birds all go into motion. The 28-gauge

Hunting Huns in the prairie foothills.

swings automatically on the closest bird, and there's a loud pop. The birds turn, flying overhead and following the creek. Not need for a second shot. After Winston's retrieve, I turn the full-grown male partridge over and over in my hand, savoring the picture-perfect flush I just witnessed. I seldom harvest more than a few birds from the two Waterfall Coveys each year, but it's nice to know they are there.

Call 'Em What You Like

The American Ornithological Union's official name for them is gray partridge, but most sportsmen know these birds as Hungarian partridge or simply as Huns. The name "Hungarian" is derived from the country where thousands of these exotic game birds were purchased for stocking in North America a century ago. But the gray partridge is also found in Europe, Asia, Scandinavia, and Great Britain and holds the distinction of being one of the most widespread game birds in the world. They're a favorite of mine, and I prefer to the call them grays or gray partridge. It just seems more descriptive of this great game bird.

In Flight, in the Hand

It's most likely that your first encounter with gray partridge will come from an explosive covey launch of ten to fifteen birds. Outside the quail family, these speedsters are the only other real covey birds in North America. They are about three times the size of bobwhites.

The gray partridge is an excellent sporting bird, but it

has a way of avoiding the game bag. When flushed, these strong, rapid, gray bullets with rusty-red tails generally take off together in tight formation and fly only a short distance, putting an obstacle between you and them before landing out of sight. Their explosive takeoff is usually accompanied by the raucous sounds of several birds calling keee-uck-kuta-kut-kut.

The gray partridge takes its common name from the bird's beautiful gray breast. The back and wings are a mottled reddish-brown and the head is colored buff and gray. It's not difficult to determine the sex. The male has a dark brown horseshoe marking on its breast, and even though some females have the same marking it's not usually as dark or well defined. Another good means of identification is the

Fully colored gray partridge.

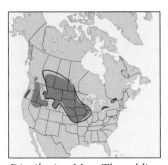

Distribution Map: The red line indicates historical range. There are many gaps within present range due to loss of habitat and human activity.

female's scapula shoulder feathers, which have a whitish line with whitish cross-barring, whereas the male's has a single whitish line and no cross-barring. An adult gray partridge tips the scales at about a pound.

For many years after its introduction the gray partridge failed to capture the imagination of most sportsmen. But today the Hun is an upland game bird that continues to grow in stature. The present geographical range of the gray partridge covers a large area of steppes and plains in North America. But not all of it includes a population density that merits a long hunting trip.

Healthy numbers of gray partridge are present in portions of North and South Dakota, Montana, Idaho, Wyoming, Saskatchewan, Alberta, and Manitoba. In many years, these states and provinces have a bumper crop and rank high in the annual number of birds harvested. In some years, good numbers of Huns are also taken in parts of British Columbia, Washington, and Oregon. There are huntable populations in some other states, as well, but for the traveling wingshooter I wouldn't recommend them. These are marginal areas, and I consider the gray partridge an incidental bird or a bonus bird that is bagged by accident when hunting another upland game bird.

Huns occupy most of the northern tier of the grassland states. This range includes agricultural land mixed within the tallgrass, mixed, and shortgrass prairies, the intermountain grasslands, and shrub grasslands. Most western grasslands of the U.S. and Canada support good populations of gray partridge, as long as habitat and food sources are available. I've even found Huns above 6,000 feet in elevation on the high plains and foothills in the shadows of the Rocky Mountains.

A Bit of History

Richard Bache is generally recognized as the first person to introduce gray partridge in North America. The place was on his estate near Beverly, New Jersey, in 1790. He transplanted pheasants at about the some time. The peasants faired better for a short time, but both were doomed to failure. The eastern terrain, habitat, climate, and the initial method of stocking all contributed to the unsuccessful establishment of an enduring population.

Pheasants continued to be transplanted in many other areas of the United States over the decades, but most were unsuccessful. But the gray partridge wasn't introduced again for over a century. For years, it was thought of as a game bird that simply couldn't adapt to the North American environment.

Most of the historical native range of the gray partridge is on the steppes of Eastern Europe and central and west-

Hunting Huns in wheat country.

ern Asia. The vast semi-arid grassland, savanna, and sagebrush plains of the Old World actually correspond well with the steppe country of North America. Both the latitude and climate are similar, and this is where the gray partridge eventually took hold in the New World.

Starting around the end of the nineteenth century, several western states and provinces released thousands of gray partridge over a period of forty years. The results in the United States were quite dismal, with only a few isolated colonies being established. Most attempts failed outright.

By far the most successful stocking program of gray partridge took place near Calgary, Alberta, in 1908 and '09. Less than two hundred pairs of birds were released in several locations, but within ten years the gray partridge population spread south and east at an unbelievable rate. This movement blanketed southern Alberta, Saskatchewan, Manitoba, and the states that border these provinces.

Despite the large numbers released by game agencies in

many of the northern states, it is fairly well documented that most of the gray partridge that now live on the Great Plains are descendants of that small stocking of birds in Alberta.

Today, over a dozen states and three provinces have established populations of gray partridge, although not always in huntable numbers.

Behavior

Knowing the daily movements and season requirements of gray partridge is a definite prerequisite for consistently finding birds in the field. The weather, the season, and the cover all have an effect on a game bird's activities, and each species reacts differently to all of these elements. Many experienced hunters doggedly hunt every game bird the same way. They work a draw or creek bottom when hunting gray partridge, just as they would for pheasants. Yet Huns are a bird of open steppes and are rarely found in heavy cover unless the canopy of woody brush and trees has no understory beneath it.

The gray partridge lives most of its life in a social group known as a covey. The yearly breakup of the covey comes as early as late January or mid-February, depending on the prevailing weather. The birds pair off after much social courtship activity. If the weather turns stormy or cold, the pairs join together again to form a loose covey for protection and roosting.

After mating, the pair stays together. Nest building takes place from late March through May, depending on latitude. The female makes her nest in suitable grassy cover with some kind of canopy of vegetation overhead. She then lays an egg every two or three days until the clutch is completed in mid-May to June. If the nest is destroyed, she will usually renest, but there will be fewer eggs.

The gray partridge has one of highest productive capacities among our game birds. The average clutch of eggs is sixteen, and it's not unusual for a hen to have over twenty. Incubation takes twenty-four days, and the peak of hatching generally occurs in early to mid-June. During the incubation period the male is always close at hand to frighten off any intruders. Both parents lead the chicks away after the last egg has hatched. The chicks' departure takes place as the day warms up, with the female in the lead, the chicks following, and the male in the rear.

Unlike with most game birds, both parents help raise the young. For the first week the chicks are brooded under the male and female at night, but as the weather warms and the young birds grow, the brood sleeps in a circle, tail-to-tail with heads pointed out. The circle provides warmth and protection from nighttime predators.

Insects are the primarily source of food from the first day of a chick's life, and they continue feeding on them as long as possible. Just like with sharptails, the first two to three weeks are critical for the birds' survival. Insects are high in protein, and the birds need this dietary component for heat, good health, and rapid development. When cold, wet weather inhibits the development of insects, chick mortality rates soar.

Once the insect population tapers off, the young birds

Gray Partridge Ground Sign

The knowledge of signs on the ground left by a gray partridge is very helpful in knowing that they are using an area to feed, roost, or loaf, and can save time in the field when looking for that species.

Tracks: look for tracks in sand, snow, mud and dirt around free water holes.

↑
1.75″
↓

Feathers: single feathers can be found in dusting, openings and roosting areas.

Single droppings: look for single droppings around riparian draws, feeding and dusting areas.

Roosting site droppings: family groups roost in one or more circles, tail to tail and leave many white and green droppings.

add tender greens and other vegetable matter to their diet. By the time gray partridge are three to four weeks, they are good strong fliers.

The brood spends much of its time in open farm fields or on grassy prairies, as long as the cover is not sparse or overgrazed. Young broods love open country, but there has to be escape cover like hedgerows, weedy ditches, overgrown fence lines, and grassy draws close by that have substantial overhead protection. Dirt lanes, dry creek washes, or open rocky areas for dusting and collecting grit must be within the general area for early morning and midday use, as well. Overall, the birds' living space has to provide food and dusting, loafing, and roosting cover.

As summer advances, the birds become adept flyers and are much more mobile and less dependent on areas with lots of edge cover. They move more freely and their coursing range expands, although it rarely exceeds a half-mile in diameter.

Fall and winter feeding is done primarily in cut grain-fields and prairie grasslands. Greens are eaten if available, but most of the birds' diet is waste grain and weed seeds. The brood still remains together, but single adults join the group and small coveys band together. Late in the year, it's possible to see twenty-five to thirty birds in a covey, but if a covey that size is flushed many times the birds break up into smaller groups. Seeing big groups late in the season is a good indication that several family units have joined together.

Living Requirements

Gray partridge require a cool and moderately dry climate. The best habitat consists of rolling hills of fertile, loamy soils, with an annual rainfall of fourteen to twenty-four inches. The Great Plains of North America fit this description perfectly, and this is where you'll find the highest density of birds.

Most hunters picture classic Hun cover as croplands with

grassy draws and shallow depressions or benchland grain-fields with brushy draws that lead into grassy sagebrush foothills with bare knolls. These places may be Hun heaven, but good Hun habitat doesn't necessarily include croplands.

For years, Huns were thought of only as a bird that lived near agricultural lands. At first this was true, but as gray partridge expanded their range they adjusted to the places of their ancestors, the uncultivated steppe country. I've hunted gray partridge not only in agricultural areas, but also in the temperate grassland ecosystem. However, covey densities in the prairie setting are usually reduced, and the birds' range is larger because the food and cover isn't as concentrated. But plenty of gray partridge live and die in the grasslands without ever seeing a kernel of grain.

Quality habitat is made up of two important cover types: cropland/grassland and brush/grassland. These two different combinations may come in many forms, such as wheatfields that have many unplowed edges, rough breaks, and grassy draws, or it may be a large section of prairie grassland, brushy draws, and woody riparian areas. Combinations of cover types are essential for Huns. Cottonwood, chokecherry, rose hips, sagebrush, and other woody cover along riparian ways and slopes and patches scattered throughout the grasslands make excellent habitat. These areas are usually found along the edges and borders of grasslands and may be greater distances apart.

Miles and miles of a single cover type, such as large wheatfields with intense clean-farming practices, leave voids

Gray Partridge and the Conservation Reserve Program

The prairie topography that seems to suit gray partridge best has deep coulees, shallow draws, and low depressions meandering through an open landscape of gently rolling hills and bare knolls. Most of the Great Plains were once like this, but over the years much of the land became tillable cropland. A lot of this land never proved very productive, so it has been included in the Conservation Reserve Program (CRP) and is now returning to grassland.

in the Hun population. Also, many acres of overgrazed rangeland are of little use to gray partridge. Both of these rural landscapes are Hun habitat disasters, and they are all too common these days.

With the exception of the first several weeks after hatching, the gray partridge is mainly a vegetarian. Both young and adults will forage on insects whenever possible, but they account for less than 10 percent of the overall diet. In summer, the birds feed mostly on leafy greens and weed seeds. If Huns live in an agricultural setting, waste grain becomes their primary food source as soon as it becomes available and for as long as it lasts. In fact, gray partridge will enlarge their range just to glean waste grains. I hunt stubble fields late in the season that have as many as ten to twelve coveys of Huns feeding in them. Once flushed, every covey goes back to its grassland draw or similar cover to hide.

Where farm crops aren't available, the Hun's main diet is a variety grass seeds and miscellaneous weed seeds. Tender greens and other leafy vegetation are eaten throughout the year, mainly in late fall and winter. Well-managed grasslands with plenty of high cover or CRP fields are ideal places for birds to find new green growth, and these areas can offer some of the best hunting late in the season.

Hunting Strategies

Gray partridge are highly prized by bird hunters. In some respects, they behave much like bobwhite quail. Both are covey birds with an explosive flush. Some hunters will tell you that bobwhites hold tighter and seldom run, but I have also found this true with Huns. Still, all game birds run; their legs are built for it and it's part of their escape anatomy. Running takes less energy than flying, and when

Rip, a hard running pointer, retrieving a Hun to Tom Petrie.

in harm's way most critters use the least amount of energy possible to escape so they can conserve power for times of imminent danger. A covey of birds is less vulnerable on the ground than in the air. And once a covey is flushed, their sole objective is to get together again as soon as possible. This is an important survival tool, as more eyes and ears aid in group protection.

The flight pattern of a covey of Huns is different from that of bobwhites. The birds stay closer together as a unit, fly farther, and seek more open habitat for landing. When bobwhites flush they go in all directions, fly only a short distance, and look for dense cover in which to hide. With Huns, you have to learn to read a larger playing field.

As mentioned earlier, the two most important cover types for gray partridge are cropfields and grasslands. But keep in mind that each one comes in many different habitat forms. No matter what else, the habitat must offer adequate year-round cover for birds. Agricultural areas are no exception; Huns can only thrive in these places if there is useable cover within or surrounding cropfields.

Grasslands are typically used to feed and raise livestock. If whole areas are intensely grazed year after year, they won't be able to sustain a healthy population of gray partridge. But if grasslands are managed properly and have good carryover cover, and change little throughout the seasons or from year to year, they have the capacity to carry good numbers of Huns. CRP has created some of the best territory because it often combines the two main habitat types, providing birds with all they need to survive on a daily and seasonal basis.

If you hunt Huns in only one of these cover types you are missing half of the places in which the birds live. My handbook for gray partridge is pretty much the same no matter where I hunt them.

Much of the grasslands I hunt remain untouched by the plow due to the lay of the land—hills, mountains, and steep slopes. Swales start on high ground and drain into draws, which contain bushy vegetation and short woody plants. The draws eventually become deeper, creating coulees that run down toward broad valleys. The coulees become wider as they drop, with steep slopes of sagebrush and juniper and grassy areas with creeks running through them. Hills with gently sloping sides often separate one coulee from another.

Hunting rolling grasslands with mixed sage is different than hunting agricultural lands. Most hunters follow the bottom of a draw to its end and then cross over to the next parallel draw, never changing elevation except within the draw itself. This method does work, but you are restricting yourself to only one small part of the landscape. Partridge frequent the bottoms only at certain times of the day and not for more than a couple of hours. They spend much more time on grassy slopes and ridges between the draws. During hot weather, with the sun blazing down, Huns are apt to be in a cool spot under a juniper, along a hillside with rock outcroppings that cast shadows, or in a shady sagebrush area.

Don't forget to factor in the weather, as bird behavior patterns change in different conditions. Also, take into account the time of year. In September, young birds feed on insects and greens in open areas. But by late November, Huns are on their winter feeding range. Look for bird sign such as feathers, droppings, and dusting places to clue you in to where the birds might be at a given time. If discovered, take into account how fresh they are.

About Dogs

Gray partridge are an open-country species, so hunting for them is a walking man's sport no matter how it's done. It's possible to hunt them without a dog, but you must walk slowly and thoroughly through cover. A good way to hunt without a dog is to drive from one known Hun hotspot to another. Huns are fond of abandoned farm building, old homesteads, and grain bins, especially after the grain harvest has been completed in early fall. In some areas on the prairies of Canada there are old buildings on crown (public) lands that you can drive to, and it's possible to have superb shooting by just walking up birds.

I use pointing dogs for hunting all prairie game bird species, and I believe Huns are tailor-made for these breeds. But no matter how you go about hunting Huns, much of the strategy I recommend below for pointing dogs will serve you well.

My preferred method is to walk the highest landforms in the area, be it a high ridge or the tops of rolling hills.

This allows me to observe the dogs working below me at a much greater distance. And it's a lot easier to walk downhill to reach a dog on point. If the birds flush before I arrive, I also have a better chance of marking them down accurately. As I walk a ridge, the dogs can make long casts on both sides, working down to the bottoms of the draws and covering all elevations, greatly

You can see in the dog's eyes how much they love to hunt Huns.

increasing their chance of finding a covey. In general, if a covey is found at a certain elevation or feeding place at a specific time of day, other coveys will be at similar elevations or locations. Always remember the elevation at which you found that first covey, as it will pay dividends throughout the day.

Once the covey is located and the pointing, shooting, and retrieving are finished, I take some mental notes. Did the birds hold tight? How many flushed? Any late singles? Were the birds flying low and in tight formation? Many times, Huns will continue to use the same maneuver on subsequent flushes.

Concentrate on the last bird to flush or the trailing bird

in the covey. It often takes the shortest route to the rendezvous point; instead of going around a hill and hooking in a different direction it will go right over the top to catch up. That last bird knows exactly where the covey is headed and will take you there on a relatively straight line.

Once you kill a Hun, examine the crop for clues to what the birds are eating. Are they feeding on greens and insects or seeds? For instance, if you find thistle seeds in the crop, scout around for thistle patches to hunt. Observe the vegetation where the first covey was flushed. Were they feeding, loafing, or dusting? Often, the flushed birds will land in the same kind of cover they were forced to leave.

If scenting conditions are good for the dogs, finding the flushed covey again should be easy. Seldom do I pursue the birds right after they're flushed, though. I like to let the birds settle in and lay down some scent. I don't usually follow the same course as the birds, but instead circle around them to give my dogs the advantage of the wind. If I'm not successful in finding the covey, I walk a circle where the first flush was made, making sure the dogs cover the whole area. By using this method, my chance of finding the covey increases tenfold. If unsuccessful again, I expand the circle. As the circle gets larger, though, the odds of finding the covey decrease.

If you have previously found a roosting area by detecting several clusters of droppings, take note. When a covey is flushed the second or third time it will break up into singles or small groups and return to a familiar site to reassemble.

Roosting places are security areas for birds, and they will often seek them out if pushed hard.

When pursuing a covey, be aware that Huns will sometimes land, feel uncomfortable, and relocate to a more desirable place. I've sometimes marked a covey down perfectly in a certain spot and then been unable to find them. I'm sure they were there, but they left for a more secure place close by.

Juvenile birds rarely flush out of shooting range, nor will they fly far. Young birds have a tendency to break from a tight formation after the second flush. This reaction is a result of the instinctive scattering chicks do when an enemy approaches. As the birds get older they stay in a compact unit longer because they are more confident in their home range.

Early in the hunting season, when the weather is warm, the dogs many have difficulty finding coveys, but this is primarily due to poor scenting conditions. I have seen days when a dog is literally standing within a covey of birds, yet is unaware of their presence. Sometimes it's so dry, with green, aromatic vegetation and no wind, that conditions are virtually useless for pointing. Scenting conditions generally improve as vegetation dies off in the fall and cooler weather prevails.

A beeper collar is a great aid for finding a rangy pointing dog in big country. I also believe a beeper collar that has a pointing mode contributes to holding birds early in the season. But later in the year a covey of Huns that has become familiar with the beeping sound may flush quickly.

Smart pointing dogs learn how to hunt Huns. Many experienced dogs that have never hunted gray partridge will get too close, pushing the birds to their limits and causing them to fly. A pointing dog that mostly hunts pheasants will also crowd Huns. If your pointing dog is hunting in big open grassland country for the first time it may take a day or two before he adjusts to any prairie bird.

Pointing dogs must learn to relocate on (not trail) moving Huns. My experienced pointers have learned to start working a covey several hundred yards away. And if scenting conditions are favorable they usually make the first point at a great distance. Once I come alongside, the dogs move ahead and point again. This can go on through several relocations. Eventually, the birds will slow up or stop and hold. The dogs know when the birds have stopped and hold as rigidly as granite rocks in a fast-flowing stream. I can always tell when the dogs are close to the birds. It shows in their eyes, and some even quiver on point.

When hunting the plains I don't want my pointers to be steady to wing and shot. As the covey flushes, the dogs learn to key in on the birds. I want them on the flying birds as soon as possible. Why lose time? If a bird is winged—Huns run when wounded—the dogs get on it quickly. Everyone goes into motion on the flush—shooters, dogs, and birds.

One of my older pointing dogs follows the covey after they've flushed. He's not chasing them, just locating the birds again. If he remains rigid after the birds flush, I know other birds are still on the ground. He is steady until the last bird leaves. (Many smart pointers learn this on their own.) He also stays rigid if birds are visible on the ground and he scents and sight-points them.

Retrievers and flushing dogs are effective when hunting Huns, but it's important to work smaller areas that have edges, like cropfields with fence lines and grassy draws. Hunting grain storage locations with close-working dogs can also net good results, because birds tend to concentrate in these places.

Hun coveys can be approached extremely close on some days. Other days, they become jumpy and are harder to get near for one reason or another. In my experience, birds that are hunted often react much sooner to an intruder and will run or flush long before danger is upon them. For this reason, I don't pursue a single covey day after day, and I rarely work a covey more than two days a week. The cover type also plays a major role in how birds respond to danger. Just remember, once you flush a covey of Huns, they can put a great distance between themselves and your second shot.

Where to Go

The heartland for gray partridge is in the central plains of North America. The highest densities occur in portions of North and South Dakota, Montana, Idaho, Wyoming, Saskatchewan, Alberta, and Manitoba. There are also good numbers of Huns in parts of British Columbia, Washington, and Oregon. The other states in which birds reside have huntable populations, but for the traveling wingshooter I wouldn't recommend going there just for Huns.

A View From the Top

It's mid-fall and the hills are golden. In the newly cultivated shelterbelt, several young gray partridge chase insects in the black earth between wide rows of Russian olives. Most of the covey is sunbathing or dusting under the canopy of leaf-less trees.

The young birds are too engaged in their favorite mid-day activity to notice my presence high above them. My vantage point gives me a near-perfect view of the entire covey. Eventually, the two adults spot me. They stir and the juveniles follow, scurrying to the next row. A windbreak is a comfort zone for covey birds, and they seldom flush through the overhead cover when pursued.

The dogs stop momentarily beside me, then run diago-nally down the slope and move into the third row of trees. I remain higher up, watching to see if my pointers, Rip and Pete, fill their nostrils with the heart-stopping scent. Rip slams to a stop first and keys in on the place the birds just left, and Pete twists his body in the same direction to honor the point.

By then, the birds have vanished beyond several rows of trees. I assume they've run out the other side of the shelter-belt into the prairie grass. I wait. No need to hurry; they won't have gone far. I arrive next to the dogs, and they relo-cate to the spot where the covey left the shelterbelt and

Gray partridge, a full-grown male.

point again. A gentle breeze drifts across the prairie, pushing even more scent toward the dogs' quivering noses and
softly stirring the gray-brown olive leaves beneath the trees.
Both pointers remain frozen like two ice sculptures at the
edge of the tilled earth, their heads held above the foot-high
golden grass.

With confidence, I move past them again and give the
signal to relocate. They move up and stop again twenty
yards in front of me.

"We have 'em," I say softly to the dogs. I can see it in
their eyes and feel the birds' presence. After three short
steps, the dogs plunge headlong into the cover. My 28-
gauge side-by-side comes up quickly. I fix my eyes on the

Sometime when hunting the high hills man and dogs have to take a break.

two dogs circling around and around in the cover as I anticipate a rush of wings. But there is nothing.

The scent seems to have vanished along with the birds. The dogs look over at me like I'm the reason the birds are gone. They certainly didn't flush, at least I don't think so. But if they had run I'm sure the dogs would have picked up their scent. I have no clue as to the birds' whereabouts, so I do the obvious and make a wide circle where I last saw the covey, then continue following the shelterbelt.

The dogs work every foot of open prairie beside the long line of trees. I think to myself, How can a whole covey of birds avoid two experienced dogs when scenting condition seem so good and every possible hiding place has been explored? Walking back to the rig along the other side of the shelterbelt, it occurs to me that the birds must have flushed when I was crossing under the trees in the shelterbelt.

After making a larger circle, we finally find them over two hundred yards from the shelterbelt in a low grassy swale. Pete catches the scent in the cool of the afternoon, and Perk follows in his footsteps and then stops. The second bird falls in an opening just as the first Hun is being retrieved.

Sometimes the shooting comes easy. But with Huns, it doesn't come often.

GREATER PRAIRIE CHICKEN
Tympanuchus cupido

Size and Weight
length: 16-19"
weight: 2-3 pounds

♂   ♀

GREATER PRAIRIE CHICKEN

Bert's Birds

The decal of a cowboy on a bucking bull above the words "Bull Durham" blocked my view through the glass door of the general store. "Do you have any rivets?" I asked the young girl behind the counter.

"What are they for?"

"I need to replace a couple of rivets in the door of one of the dog compartments on my hunting rig. The rattle reminds me to get it fixed every time I drive down a rough road in this farm country. I have a little time before the weather clears this morning and I go hunting, so I thought this would a good time to get it fixed."

"Have a cup of coffee," she said with a smile, "I'll go look, but I don't remember seeing any."

"Nope," she continued, walking back. "I suggest you go to Bert's Welding Shop."

"Well it's not much of a job," I said. "I don't want to bother anyone with such a simple task that I can do myself."

"Oh, Bert won't mind. And furthermore, he loves hunting dogs. Bert would rather talk dogs and hunting than work. I'll bet when he sees your hunting rig, he'll fix the door just to see the dogs."

Diet Icons for Prairie Chickens

Habitat Icons for Prairie Chickens

"Thanks for the coffee and the help," I said, backing out the door.

"Have a good hunt," she said, and then waved.

Fixing the door was easy, thanks to Bert's pop rivet gun. Then I showed him the five Brittanys I had with me.

"It's no fun hunting chickens without pointing dogs," Bert said. "I had a German shorthair, but she died when I was gone. After I got back from Vietnam, I started this business and moved to town. Training another pointing dog just didn't fit into my schedule. I sure wish I had one. I will one of these days."

"Bert, this is my last day here. Would you like to come along and see the dogs work? I'm going to a walk-in area west of here that's had very good chicken hunting."

"I'll take a rain check," he said laughing, "I've got too much going on today."

Bert lived in small friendly town in South Dakota. After his father passed away, he leased his family's two farms and his mother moved into town. He hadn't done much hunting since his old dog had died, other than going after pheasants with a buddy who owned a Labrador retriever.

It wasn't until the next year that I got to know Bert on a personal basis.

"Ben," he told me on the phone, "if you want to shoot some chickens, we can hunt my two farms. There are usually four or five flocks on the home place that feed in the alfalfa field in the morning and spend the rest of the day in the hills. The other farm has more woody draws and there are a lot of sharptails, but I've seen chickens in the low hills there, too."

"Good," I said, "I'm looking for prairie chickens. I have plenty of sharptails here at home."

"We'll meet opening day of grouse season at the old home place, Ben. I'm having the old two-story farmhouse fixed up and painted so we'll have a nice place to stay. Follow the directions I gave you and you can't miss the white house and big red barn. See you soon."

So now I'm driving through the rolling farm fields not far from Bert's place. All the farmhouses I've passed look the same. Most were built just after the turn of the century, and the architectural plans are right out of an old Sears & Roebuck catalog. I'm thinking, The general store must sell a lot of red and white paint. All the houses are newly painted white, and the barns red. I notice that the old red tractors are all of the same vintage. Must have had a good Farmall dealer in the region.

A newly painted two-rail white fence surrounds the lawn

of the next two-story farmhouse. I'm sure this is Bert place, but he didn't mention the white fence. It's the only thing that's different from all the other farms I've driven by.

The note on the back door confirms that it's his. "Ben, I have to work late, so I can hunt with you for the next couple of days. Marge, the tenant's wife, put supper in the fridge for you. Make yourself at home. See you at breakfast. Bert."

Over bacon, eggs, and hash browns the next morning, Bert starts talking first.

"Ben, ever since I was a kid, hunting here for chickens has always involved the same routine. Skip, my German shorthair, and I would walk the edges of the hayfield first and see if any birds were still feeding. I always had my doubts, but invariably a young bird or two would linger there. Why, I don't know. Then I would…"

He stopped, took a sip of coffee, looked at me, and asked, "Ben, however you want to hunt is fine with me. You know your dogs and have hunted chicken in a lot of different locations."

"Bert, that doesn't mean I know how to hunt your place. I suggest we use your plan, you know the lay of the land and where the birds were in the past. Bird patterns don't change much from year to year unless the habitat has changed. Have the farming practices changed now that you have a tenant on the homestead?" I asked.

"No. In fact, I think the bird habitat is better. I know that's true for pheasants. We have a lot more cover today than when I lived here."

When we leave the house the sun is just breaking over the highest hills, warming up the side hills where the birds will soon be taking their sunlight baths.

I drive down the lane and stop. Bert wrestles the barbed-wire gate open and I drive into the hayfield. I pull up next to the haystack and park.

Bert shruggs his shoulders, not looking at me, then says, "The meadow's cut short. I don't think a chicken in its right mind would use this field."

I get out and walk to the haystack, looking for chicken sign. Bert follows. Bird droppings and feathers are everywhere. "They're here," I say, scraping the ground with my boot.

Bert clears his throat. "I'll be darned. Do you think they're using the hayfield, too?"

"Yeah, they sure are," I say, looking across the barren field. "But I'll tell you this, when they do, you will never get close to them. What's the best way to get to those hills where the sun is just coming over?"

"Straight ahead, follow the edge of the field. But go slow, Ben, this hayfield is rough."

We bounce down the cut field, following the fence. Three half-grown rooster pheasants run ahead of us, their plumage still resembling a hen's. They cut into the heavy cover along the dilapidated wooden posts and woven-wire fence.

"I hope the hills aren't full of young pheasants. The dogs will spend all day pointing running pheasants. You know, Bert, pheasants can ruin a good pointing dog."

Beyond the hayfield the land lifts to join the hills. The

bunchgrass and scattered silver sage catch my eye first. The prairie waves its golden hair and glistens in the sun.

"Nice cover, Bert. It's the best I've seen for prairie chickens around here."

"Ben, these are the hills where I use to hunt, but I usually drove on a sandy two-track road that goes up that long hill to the right and follows the ridge for a mile until it dips back down the other side. We'll go back that way. It's a lot less bumpy."

I let three Brittanys out of the dog compartments and put beepers on them as Bert slides the shotguns out of their leather cases. When it comes to hunting prairie grouse, I prefer a light 28-gauge side-by-side. Bert carries a Browning Superposed over/under 12-gauge.

We are a hundred yards below the ridge when the dogs disappear over the top. Not long after, we hear the beepers sounding the hawk scream—dogs on point. I scurry toward the horizon just as two birds appear dark against the morning sky, sailing overhead and then down the slope before disappearing in the golden grass. Once on top, I wait for Bert, watching the three dogs still on point.

"Bert, the Britts are right below us. Catch your breath, they won't move."

"What a nice sight, all three dogs strung out in a line. Who's the lead dog?" Bert asked.

"It's Pat. He's only nine months old, but he'll hold them." We hurried down the slope, walking past Mac, then Terra, before stopping behind Pat.

Prairie chickens are birds of big open grasslands.

"Go ahead, Bert, but slowly," I said, and wave him on.

Bert looks over at me, but I shake my head and motion him on.

Bert passes in front of Pat, and the other two dogs break. Seven chickens feather the light breeze and turn downwind. Two shots ring out, and feathers drift slowly down as Mac and Terra retrieve the brace of barred birds.

"Nice shooting, Bert," I say, shaking his hand. I mark the others down.

"Why didn't you walk in and shoot, Ben?"

"Sometimes it's just fun to see the overall picture of man, dogs, and birds all in motion. And I know where the other birds went. Let's go get them."

Call 'Em What You Like

Beyond a doubt, the pinnated grouse is the prairie game bird most associated with the westward movement of settlers across the Great Plains. The wild chicken was the "people's bird." It came and went like many sodbusters, who had more than a few names for it.

The pinnated grouse was variously known as the prairie cock, prairie hen, squaretail, boomer, fool hen, wild chicken, barred grouse, or yellowlegs. Today, in areas where pinnated grouse live in harmony with sharp-tailed grouse, local folks just call them "chickens" and "grouse," respectively, although traveling wingshooters typically stick to the name prairie chicken.

In Flight, in the Hand

Prairie chickens are often found in habitat that also harbors sharptails. If you are only after chickens, here are some distinctive characteristics that will help you differentiate between the two species. Both flush similarly, but once airborne, a chicken's wing beats are slower and the wings less cupped. From the side, the top of the chicken's wings appear almost flat in flight, not curved like a sharptail's. In fact, their wing beat and appearance more closely resembles a domestic pigeon in flight. Chickens also appear much darker in comparison to the whitish color of the sharptail, and chickens sometimes cackle when flushed, while sharptails cluck. After you've seen both birds on the wing, it won't be difficult to distinguish between them.

Pheasants are present in many places that chickens live, as well, and a hen pheasant can sometimes confuse the hunter. In most states, prairie grouse and pheasant hunting seasons don't start at the same time, and hens are protected anyway, so it's important to learn all upland game bird flight patterns in a given area. Be careful, and always make a quick identification before shooting.

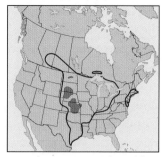

Distribution Map: The red line indicates historical range. There are many gaps within present range due to loss of habitat and human activity.

A pheasant usually runs and flushes horizontal to the ground, and its wings look straighter. Both chickens and sharptails push off vertically and frequently flush in small groups. Another point to remember is that a pheasant in flight looks like a torpedo with a long pointed tail, while the prairie chicken has a round tail and appears plumb.

In hand, both sexes of greater prairie chicken are alike in color. The upper parts are brownish, and the breast and belly are a light buff color with dark brown cross-barring. (Sharptails have distinctive V-shaped markings on the breast instead of bars.) The tail of the prairie chicken is short and round, the legs and feet are feathered to the toes, and the feet are yellow.

The adult male weighs about 2 1/2 pounds and has long

stiff feathers called "pinnae" on the side of the neck, hence the name "pinnated grouse." Males also have a small yellow comb above the eye and two yellow-orange air sacs on each side of the neck.

The female is a little smaller in size and lighter in weight. Both sexes of lesser prairie chicken are smaller than the greater and a little lighter in color, but the overall look is very similar. The two species are easily confused, but their ranges don't overlap.

The current distribution of the pinnated grouse is quite different from its historic range. It was once one of the most plentiful native game birds in North America, thriving in the savanna habitat of the central part of the continent. Sadly, it has been severely affected by human activity through the years.

There are four subspecies of pinnated grouse, include the heath hen, which is now extinct. Its range extended along both the northeast and south-central coasts. The Attwater's prairie chicken is an endangered species that once lived in a large portion of southern Texas and Louisiana. It is now restricted to a small area of southeast Texas. The lesser prairie chicken once thrived in several south-central states. Today, it has only a limited population in small portions of Texas and Kansas.

The greater prairie chicken lived in great numbers in the open grassland country from southern Canada down to Texas and from Colorado to eastern Ohio. But for many years this wonderful game bird has been extinct across much of its original range. These days, only three states still have excellent populations, while a few other states have a limited number of birds.

Even though it is still possible to hunt the lesser prairie chicken in a few areas, the greater prairie chicken is the main focus of this chapter. But, of course, the information provided here also applies to lesser prairie chickens.

A Bit of History

The overall range of the four subspecies of pinnated grouse once stretched from Vermont down the eastern coast to

Georgia and from British Columbia and Alberta south to New Mexico. The heath hen was the first species encountered by colonists in Massachusetts and Virginia. It was not a woodland grouse, but a bird indigenous to a narrow band of scrub oak plains.

Though once very common, humans virtually destroyed the bird's habitat. And by the late 1800s the heath hen had become extinct on the mainland, with only a remnant population on Martha's Vineyard. With the help of the state of Massachusetts and several private organizations, several hundred acres were purchased to protect the heath hen from extinction. But it was too late. After a number of catastrophic events, the last heath hen died in 1931. Fortunately, the pinnated grouse had three other subspecies that still lived over a large range of North America for quite some time.

When early settlers advanced to the Midwest the greater prairie chicken was as numerous as the buffalo. It was thought that with so much favorable prairie habitat the abundance of chickens would last forever.

At first, only part of the vast big and little bluestem prairie came under the plow, and the prairie chicken adapted well to its new way of life. But the Midwest soon became the breadbasket for a fast-growing nation, and most of the native prairie was eventually put into production. Prairie chickens require substantial amounts of grasslands for their daily and yearly needs, and when the prairie grasses disappeared so did most of the greater prairie chickens.

Prairie chicken booming on its lek (breeding grounds).

The grouse did manage to hang on in some areas where adequate grasslands were available, but by the turn of the last century their booming grounds fell silent across many of the states and all of the provinces in which the birds once lived.

Behavior

Many habits of the prairie chicken are similar to those of sharp-tailed grouse. Both birds gather on breeding grounds called leks, although the mating rituals are quite different. Their courtships are unique and marvelous. Sharptail leks are also called dancing grounds because the males go through a dance ritual to attract females. Prairie chickens leks are known as booming grounds because they go through a booming ritual to do the same.

Each prairie chicken cock displays individually in his special small territory among many other grouse. The ritual begins with a short run and a quick stop. The bird then stamps his feet on the ground, sometimes rotating around. Then he raises his pinnae and inflates the orange air sacs on his neck. With tail open and wings dropped, he makes a booming sound created by a resonant effect of the air sacs.

Observing a lek when mating activity begins in March and April—whether watching prairie chickens boom, sharptails dance, or sage grouse strut—is an experience you'll never forget.

Once courtship is complete, the prairie chicken's reproductive, nesting, brooding, and rearing habits are very similar to the sharp-tailed grouse. The prairie chicken is prolific, with a clutch size ranging from ten to sixteen eggs. Incubation requires twenty-three days. The eggs hatch over a period of just a day, and as soon as the last chick is dry the female leads the young away from the nest.

The rate of growth and life cycle are almost identical to the sharptail. The young birds develop very rapidly, and within four weeks they can fly short distances. For the first two weeks the chicks feed primarily on insects, but various greens and seeds soon become their dominant food sources.

As the poults get older their needs vary from day to day, but the basic requirements for food, moisture, dusting, roosting, lofting, and social interaction stay the same.

Prairie chickens are early risers, off the roost before sunup. They typically fly to feed each morning and evening, but sometimes stay in the fields throughout the midday hours if the weather is overcast or stormy. When the weather is clear the flocks feed for a couple of hours and then hit the slopes below the higher grassland ridges to loaf, chase grasshoppers, sun, and preen themselves. Prairie chickens prefer these places for several reasons: they can look out across the prairie for danger, the slopes facing the sun warm up first, and there's less vegetation so hinder movement. These open areas also provide good dusting spots. Chickens don't like to get wet, and the sunny slopes quickly shed the morning dew. The birds spend much of the day resting in the scattered patches of thin cover.

Before sundown, chickens fly into their roosting areas in a loose flock. These areas must include fairly high grass and abundant cover. The birds scatter after landing and roost in a loose cluster.

Living Requirements

Reading the habitat and learning the birds' habits are the keys to finding them in open country. I believe prairie chickens are more predictable than sharptails in their daily and seasonal movements because the habitat they prefer has less variety. The one important cover type required by prairie chickens is grassland. When large blocks of it are available, the birds can find everything they need to thrive.

The best grasslands for chickens include rolling hills,

knolls, ridges, and swales with different types and density of grassy cover. A rolling topography has more soil variation, and these, in turn, support many different types of vegetation.

Despite the massive habitat destruction of the last century, it's still possible to experience the grandeur of the Great Plains while hunting the big and little bluestem grasslands. There is still good habitat for prairie chickens. Great stretches of the prairie have been rehabilitated into national grasslands, mostly in the Dakotas. And because of their topography, places like the Flint Hills of Kansas and the Sandhill country of Nebraska still have millions of acres of prairie that are grazed to varying degrees.

Also, there are areas of the Great Plains that were never suited for optimum cropland use. Some acreages were never plowed and other were eventually abandoned. Wild hayfields and pasturelands have taken the place of native grasslands and some are still acceptable to prairie chickens. Grasslands with reasonable grazing practices and moderate hay harvests can be important prairie chicken cover.

Generally, at least 40 percent of the land must be suitable grassland cover for prairie chickens to survive. The higher the percentage of grass, the better, but it must be available in large parcels, not small, scattered units. Grasslands of one type or another match every need of the prairie chicken throughout the year. The balance of the land can be in grain and areas of brushy cover or swales. If scattered around or surrounded by large areas of grasslands, grainfields become an important element of good prairie chicken habitat.

Autumn brings great change in the prairie chicken's diet, with the bulk shifting to vegetable matter. Before croplands became part of the landscape, prairie chickens predominantly ate greens, a variety of seeds, wild fruits, and insects. But today cereal grains are their favorite foods, as long as these are available within the birds' coursing range.

By late fall and winter the chickens are mostly eating waste grains. Birds join together at this time of year, and big flocks expand their range in search of food.

Hunting Strategies

As discussed above, prairie chickens like large areas of unbroken prairie with native grasses and weeds that haven't been overgrazed. They prefer the wide-open spaces of tree-less, rolling plains. Heavy brush and trees are not used by prairie chickens.

Early in the day, look for birds in uncut or high-cut croplands adjacent to or within large grasslands, where they like to feed. If grain is available, that's where you'll find them early morning and again before they roost at sun-down. Once their crops are full of grain, they loaf in grassy hangouts close by.

After the sun warms the grasslands, the prairie is the best place to find chickens. But where they go within these areas depends on the amount of cover available. As a rule, chickens prefer to use unbroken rolling prairie, the sunny slopes

A brace of prairie chickens.

of hillsides, or the highest landforms available to sun themselves or loaf after feeding. These areas tend to have sparser cover so birds can move around more freely.

Knowing that they tend to hold up after feeding, I walk the sunny slopes of low hills first, and then work both sides of the ridges later on. When I find birds at a certain elevation or in a specific type of cover, I continue to hunt similar areas for the next hour or so.

Chickens often move to heavy cover at lower elevations when the hills heat up through the middle of the day. I've had the best results at midday by working large grasslands and low grassy swales and draws.

Like all game birds, prairie chickens will feed occasionally throughout the day. So no matter what time of day you shoot your first bird, take a crop sample to see what seeds or greens it has been eating. This information may help you determine where birds were feeding before the flush or even earlier that morning, which may be useful the following day. I once found a large amount of ragweed seeds in the crop of a bird I had just shot. The rest of that day and the next, I made it a point to hunt ragweed patches. And I was well rewarded.

Be aware of everything around you while hunting. Look for droppings, feathers, dusting sites, roosting areas, and birds on the move. All of these are good indicators of how birds are using certain areas at different times during the day.

In most states, the prairie chicken season starts in mid-September. Family groups are still together and hold well at this time. By early October, the birds start to band together in large flocks and become much more wary and difficult to approach. As the season progresses, they also increase their range in search of food and become more nomadic. As winter draws near, cut grainfields with little cover are the birds' favorite feeding areas. But it's almost impossible to get near the large flocks.

The first few weeks of the hunting season definitely offer the best shot opportunities, but if you're planning to hunt a well-known public grassland I would advise skipping opening weekend because of the large number of hunters afield. After the first few days, you'll more than likely have most of the grouse cover to yourself.

About Dogs

During the first three or four weeks of the hunting season, chickens hold well for dogs and flush at close range. And when hunting the open prairie, dogs certainly help with finding, flushing, and retrieving birds.

Sometimes it all comes together when your dog retrieves his first prairie chicken.

Many experienced hunters use flushing dogs to hunt both prairie chickens and sharptails, but to be effective the dogs must hunt close. A good flushing dog can put a lot of birds in the air within shooting range. The only disadvantage of using a close-working dog is that it just can't cover a lot of country like a big-running pointing dog.

As with all game birds in open country, I prefer to hunt with pointing dogs. Young chickens in good grassy cover behave very well for pointing dogs. But an inexperienced pointing dog must quickly learn not to crowd birds.

A pointing dog that has been trained on pen-raised birds won't do very well at first. But a dog with good instincts picks up the routine quickly. The dog that hunts only wild running pheasants also may have trouble holding chickens. Whatever the breed, the dog must learn to be more cautious when pointing prairie chickens.

Every species of game bird has to be approached differently with a pointing dog, and prairie chickens are no exception. Chickens are flock birds, but they tend to spread out in small groups in the grasslands. So dogs are generally pointing just one or two birds instead of the whole flock. To be successful, your dog must learn to point the birds at some distance. Like sharptails, chickens cannot be hunted day after day and still be expected to hold for a dog. Open-country birds become very wary when pushed too often.

Where To Go

For the past few decades, state and federal wildlife agencies have made great strides in rehabilitating habitat and securing new lands for the recovery of good populations of prairie chickens. Still, these fine birds of the grasslands are currently found in only a few regions. The best hunting for greater prairie chickens is in South Dakota, Nebraska, and Kansas. Colorado and Minnesota have very limited hunting. Lesser prairie chickens can be hunted in Texas and Kansas, but their numbers are quite small.

In states where hunting is allowed, the birds are found only in certain locations. So when planning a trip to hunt chickens it's best to contact state game authorities to get updated information. Chambers of commerce or tourist agencies can also be very helpful in pinpointing good areas for the traveling wingshooter.

Thinking Back

The dogs had a different idea than we did. With their beepers sounding, they disappeared in a draw full of tall grass to search for pheasants. Several big roosters came boiling out a hundred yards ahead before I could get the dogs turned in our direction.

"The dogs have to have fun too, Ben," Bert said, laughing. "And I thought you said you knew where those other chickens went after coming off the hill."

"Well, Bert, the dogs got a little sidetracked with those darn roosters. The last time I saw those five chickens they were flying low. And just before the birds landed I saw a flash of wings in the sun just beyond the patch of grass the pheasants came out of. They should be another three hundred yards beyond the grassy swale, halfway up that low hill ahead of us."

As we walked along, with all three dogs running in front, the hill ahead reminded me of the first place I hunted chickens years ago. Prairie chickens have stayed in the back of my mind ever since. They've become an important game bird for me, although not for the killing. I won't take a limit of chickens in a single day.

I acquired this special feeling for the birds the first time I hunted old yellowlegs. Driving in South Dakota during the heat of the day, I stopped several times to let the dogs

Hunting chickens with a small Munsterlander on big Nation Grasslands just goes together.

get a drink and exercise. For miles in every direction, I saw tall golden sun-baked grass swirling to the horizon. I figured I'd better hunt early the next morning before the sun fried the earth. It was really too hot for good hunting, but I wanted to find a few prairie chickens.

It was already after eight o'clock on the first day when I talked to Wilber Franks, who was standing next to three vintage orange tractors, two of which didn't run. Will's "eighty," the old family homestead, never passed into government hands and was surrounded by public grasslands. I got his name from an auctioneer, who said, "Will never outgrew the way he grew up. He learned about chickens as a kid and still bids on old tractor parts that were once orange."

"Now you want chickens, not grouse?" Will asked. "You want them barred, the ones with yellow feet."

I explained that I knew the difference between speckled bellies and barred bellies.

Wilber half smiled, looking down at a pile of junk, then said, "Most city folks haven't learned the ways of birds or keeping stuff. I never throw anything away that might someday have a use. And I no longer have time to hunt chickens like when I was growing up."

Looking toward the grasslands, he pointed, then looked at his watch. "Well," he said, "I see you have a couple of bird dogs. Just take them toward that grassy draw and hunt the other side where it's sunny. They should be there by now."

He glanced down at his watch again and continued, "I never hunted until after chores. The best place is in grass, chickens won't hold in cut grain anyway. If time allowed, I'd go with you."

He didn't make a big thing of going, though. With a thousand old used parts laying in front of him, most of them painted orange, Will's mind was focused on fixing something. I'm sure bird hunting hadn't crossed his mind in years.

I had the pleasure of getting to know Wilber Franks well before he died, and he was right about the chickens being on that sunny hillside on the day we first met. Through our conversations, he taught me a lot about how to hunt old yellowlegs.

But I had to shake off my reverie, because within a hundred yards all three dogs stopped. Bert was ahead and to my left. Before I could move up, two birds flushed and swung past Bert. His shotgun came up automatically and the first bird rolled to a stop at his feet. The other one sailed on down the hill, and then curved to follow the swale. Two more birds thundered straight away from me, going hell-bent for the top of the hill. Sometimes a shotgun seems to work as if by magic, and the perfect double materializes out of nowhere. But, then again, we seem to forget the easy shots.

SAGE GROUSE
Centrocercus urophasianus

Size and Weight
MALE
length: 28-31"
weight: 5-7 pounds

FEMALE
length: 20-23"
weight: 3-4 pounds

SAGE GROUSE

Meadow Creek

Pete once showed me a map of the original ranch on Meadow Creek that his father had drawn for him not long after he bought the entire place. His father, Ray, had married a hometown girl whose brother managed a huge sheep operation in Idaho. He became the ranch foreman for his brother-in-law until he partnered up with an uncle, Frank, in Montana.

Frank homesteaded and then purchased other sections—a section is 640 acres—surrounding his land through delinquent tax sales. After several dry years there wasn't enough grass for the number of sheep needed to support the place. He got overextended and the business was about to go belly up when Ray stepped in and bought the homestead and half the holdings.

Frank soon came to hate Ray, but no one could say they didn't work hard together. Ray and his wife, Clara, move into the white, two-story house Frank had built himself. Being a bachelor, Frank moved into the mouse-infested bunkhouse. Ray simply knew a lot more about sheep and how to manage a big spread than his uncle, and that didn't go over too well. The fact that Ray had a wife, a team of draft horses, and money in the bank didn't help their relationship, either.

So after two miserable years in business together, Ray bought out his uncle. Frank moved to town and purchased a blacksmith shop. Ray never stepped foot in the shop, nor did Frank ever come out to the ranch again.

Ray's plan was to build several dams, one for irrigation and the others for livestock, in each section that didn't have a permanent water source. After two more years of hard work with a horse and bucket, Ray completed an irrigation ditch and two small stock dams. The next year he got two cutting of hay from the irrigated land. He put up enough alfalfa hay to feed his stock all winter. He also bought more summer pasture, good sagebrush-grassland country, and leased several other sections of BLM land next to the ranch.

When Ray got too old to work the place he turned the ranch over to his son. Pete learned the sheep business and never deviated from his dad's rotation cycle or his irrigation plan. The only thing Pete did differently was to get a used tractor to cut and stack hay and an old truck for ranch work. Pete got married not long after his dad died, but most folks surmised that it was more to acquire a ranch hand than a wife.

Pete rotated the sheep to high pasture in summer, wintered them along the creek, and kept them on the home section during lambing—just like his father had done. It was widely believed that no other man in the country knew more about raising sheep than Ray.

Pete said, "When the time came to sell, my dad always

Diet Icons for Sage Grouse

Habitat Icons for Sage Grouse

anticipated the number of sheep the place could carry the next year. He never overextended that capacity or harmed the land."

Several years before I first met Pete, he had gotten out the sheep business and started raising Black Angus with the same success. And the overall ranch operation stayed exactly the same.

Thanks to his land-management practices, Pete's place was an upland bird hunting paradise. His ranch had by far the best bird population in the area, but back then most folks hunted only big game. Hunting prairie game birds was almost unheard of.

Getting permission to hunt birds on Pete's land was easy. He told me no one had ever asked him before.

"You want to hunt what?" he asked.

"Game birds," I answered. "I have two dogs with me and we can walk from here."

"What kind of dogs are they?"

"Brittanys."

"Never heard of them," Pete said, and then walked over

to look in the small back window of the Volkswagen. "Nice-looking dogs. What do they do?"

"They're pointing dogs."

"Never seen a dog point. Like to see them sometime."

"You are certainly welcome," I said.

"Oh, one of these days I will," he said. "What kind of birds are you after?"

"Sage hens today."

"Yah, there's always a bunch of those big brown chickens along the edge of the hayfield early morning when I go to check on the heifers. If I get too close, the males fly toward the big sagebrush flat. But the young ones don't even move when I drive by. My dad called them fool hens. Do you eat them?"

"Sure do, the young birds are very good, Pete."

"Help yourself, but don't bring me any."

Pete's ranch buildings lay scattered along both sides of Meadow Creek, below the old white house that was badly in need of a coat of paint. The creek ran through the split-rail juniper corral that Pete and his wife cut and hauled from the mountains a truckload at a time.

Two blue-black ranch dogs escorted the Volkswagen from the house and continued to bark until I crossed the little wooden bridge. I followed a two-track that paralleled the creek for a half-mile and parked next to the diversion dam at the edge of a cut hayfield.

I first caught sight of the birds in the alfalfa field not far from the irrigation ditch that separated the hayfield from an

In sage grouse country, the more dogs the better.

unbroken sagebrush slope. Pete's place is rugged, strong, and unforgiving country. It lies in the shadow of the Rocky Mountains, where chinook winds and thunderstorms roll across the landscape, unexpectedly appearing and disappearing like the sage grouse themselves. For me, these magnificent birds and the land they occupy hold a magic that's inexpressible.

I actually saw my first sage grouse many years earlier when glassing a large sagebrush basin for mule deer in central Washington. Back then, sage hens were mysterious to me. I found them to be big enchanting birds, residents of miles of purple sage where fences were few and failed homesteads many.

Looking out over Pete's place, I saw the shadows of large

cumulus clouds passing slowly over the meadow. As long as I've known Pete, he's never gotten a third cutting of alfalfa off that meadow. A few scattered plants were topped with the last blue flowers of the season, but most of the field was still cut short from the second mowing.

I saw little bunches of sage grouse family groups scattered throughout the alfalfa field. Several big adult males appeared nervous at the sight of my blue Bug, but the others never stopped feeding.

I stepped out of the vehicle and the two Brittanys piled out behind me, almost knocking me down. At once, all the birds became nervous and their heads came up. They slowly flushed group by group and disappeared into the sea of sage. The dogs were eager to go, so we moved into the huge field of aromatic cover. It didn't take long. Two five- or six-pound birds were enough.

Looking back, I've hunted Pete's land for almost half a century, but I've never had a desire to take a limit of these special birds.

Call 'Em What You Like

Members of the Lewis & Clark expedition named them "cock of the plains." Others who followed called them sage chickens, sage hens, or sage cocks. Latecomers used even more descriptive names, like spiny-tailed pheasant, fool hen, and, more recently, prairie bomber. Today, most of us that hunt this grand game bird call them by the name that fits best—sage grouse.

In Flight, in the Hand

Other than wild turkey, sage grouse are the largest gallinaceous bird in North America. A big adult male has a wingspan of over three feet, measures thirty inches in length, and tips the scales at over seven pounds. No wonder some hunters call them prairie bombers. They sound like thunder when flushed and create large shadows on the prairie.

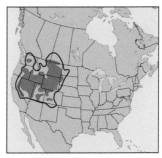

Distribution Map: The red line indicates historical range. There are many gaps within present range due to loss of habitat and human activity.

Their big bodies, dark color, pointed tails, and distinctive sagebrush habitat make it easy to identify sage grouse on the wing. No other game bird takes off in such ungainly fashion, but once airborne sage grouse accelerate quickly, their wings dipping from side to side as they alternately pound the air then glide again and again.

In hand, sage grouse are magnificent in color and impressive in size. Both sexes are similar. The bird is basically graybrown, with a dark belly. The male is mostly brown on the upper body with lighter spots and bars on the wings and tail. The bird's breast is white, with thin black streaks and scalelike feathers, and it has a long, stiff, spiny tail. The female is much smaller, but has the same general color pattern.

The landscape of the intermountain states was once an

A large male sage grouse is considered a trophy bird.

ocean of diverse sagebrush flora. And the sage grouse was originally found wherever sagebrush was plentiful. This semiarid habitat originally occurred in thirteen states and two provinces, and all had good populations of sage grouse. The area extended from the southern edge of Saskatchewan and Alberta to the northern parts of New Mexico and from parts of California, Oregon, and Washington east to the western side of the Dakotas and Nebraska.

But drought, overgrazing, and intensive agriculture have greatly altered the sagebrush community and eliminated populations across much of the historical range. By the 1930s, the big grouse was no longer a major upland game bird species in many areas. Sage grouse are still relatively secure in nine states, but hunting is by permit only or heavily regulated in over half of these.

A Bit of History

Long before the westward movement of European settlers, sage grouse played a part in the nomadic culture of Native

American. Historical evidence suggests that sage grouse were an important part of their food supply, decorations, and spiritual rituals. Sage grouse remains have been found in numerous prehistoric Indian sites. The Lewis & Clark expedition is credited with recording the first sighting of sage grouse, in the vicinity of the Marias River in northern Montana. The men encountered large flocks of grouse as they continued west.

Sage grouse were originally found wherever pioneers and homesteaders settled in intermountain sagebrush country. As the birds were so abundant, no one ever thought it possible that they could be decimated, but by the end of the nineteenth century it became obvious that human encroachment was having a serious effect on the birds' environment. In some areas, quality habitat was completely eliminated. But back then, it was not fully understood that sage grouse were totally dependent on sagebrush for food and cover year-round.

In the late 1940s and early '50s, restricted grazing practices were implemented on public lands, and that program alone helped in reestablishing livable habitat that could once again support good numbers of sage grouse.

Over half of all sagebrush communities have already been lost, though, and what remains has been severely altered. Part of the reason for this decline has been an attitude in the West that sagebrush is a hindrance to agricultural, something that needs to be removed by burning, spraying, and plowing.

Sage Grouse Ground Sign

The knowledge of signs on the ground left by a sage grouse is very helpful in knowing that they are using an area to feed, roost, or loaf, and can save time in the field when looking for that species.

Tracks: look for tracks in sand, snow, mud, power dirt and around watering holes.

male

female

Single droppings: look for single droppings in open sagebrush areas and around water holes.

Roosting site droppings: family groups roost individually, but in the same proximity, called clusters.

Feathers: single feathers can be on the ground, hanging in sagebrush and around waterholes.

At present, there is a growing concern over the long-term forecast for all kinds of wildlife associated with sagebrush in the intermountain west. State and federal wildlife agencies are now working hard to restore habitat suitable for the birds' survival and to sustain huntable populations in areas that have seen dramatic decreases.

Behavior

A female sage grouse flies into a clearing on a large sagebrush flat in eastern Montana just minutes after an April sunrise.

She walks toward the center of the clearing and approaches several big male grouse. The males are at the peak of courting fervor. She joins three more females in the inner circle. The males begin their strutting performance. They dash forward with their wings out and huge air sacs bouncing. The birds contract their neck muscles and the sacs resound with plopping sounds that can be heard for a mile.

Mating activity is centered on a lek, or strutting ground, in early spring and can include anywhere from twenty to several hundred birds. After mating takes place, nesting occurs in a sagebrush community over the next two or three weeks. The female lays six to ten eggs and incubation requires twenty-five days. The chicks are led from the nest a few hours after their down has dried. The hen takes complete care of the young chicks for about two months. As with other game birds that use leks, the male has no association with the young. The mother teaches her chicks to feed and escape danger. For the first several week of the chicks' life insects are the main diet.

Young sage grouse have a much looser association with the hen than other game bird chicks. And if other broods are in the same area the chicks may shift and join another family group. So it's possible for a hen to end up with more chicks than she hatched.

The chicks learn to fly within several weeks, but the brood stays close together throughout the summer. By late August, the families begin to break up into mixed groups, and by September a complete shuffle takes place that leaves

Two male sage grouse strutting on a lek (breeding ground).

them little contact with their mother. Young sage grouse don't become completely mature until November.

Flocking begins by late fall, and the groups can get quite large. As flocks merge together, many immature males also rejoin the groups. Older males usually keep to themselves. At this time, large concentrations of birds become very nomadic and can range great distances to find food. Despite their awkward takeoff, sage grouse are strong fliers.

The birds are early risers, usually going to water not long after sunrise. They don't need it every day, though, as dew or snow also slakes their thirst. Feeding areas and water sources are not necessarily close together, and at times they may be great distances apart.

Once the birds' crops are full they find a place to rest and dust if the weather is warm. If it's cold they move to open areas to sun themselves. By early afternoon the birds get restless and again go to feed, and they'll often have another drink if water is available. Sage grouse go to roost in late evening and settle down on the ground in loose clusters. They are well camouflaged and roost in fairly open sage-brush cover.

Living Requirements

Unlike many of our other game birds, sage grouse are locked into a single ecosystem year-round. They are native to the sagebrush-grassland steppe of intermountain North America. This habitat includes arid low basin prairie all the way to the foothills of the high mountains. Elevations run from 2,000 to 8,000 feet and rainfall and temperature vary greatly.

Most of the good sage grouse range is in sagebrush-grass-land prairie habitat. The rest is salt-desert shrub habitat, which also gets used, although not as extensively. These two habitat types are usually separate, but they may be mixed in some areas due to the soil types present.

The salt-desert brush habitat is much more arid than typical sagebrush-grassland; its rainfall rarely exceeds ten inches. The soil is generally poor and not suitable for agri-culture, which means it's less likely to be plowed under. But sage grouse don't take to this habitat as readily because the cover is thinner and shorter.

Basically, sage grouse are only found where sagebrush is

plentiful. Different size and cover types within this sage-brush-grassland prairie community are vital for meeting the birds' year-round requirements. Sage grouse need breeding, nesting, brood-rearing, and winter habitat to survive. If one of these habitats within a large sagebrush community is removed or destroyed, the birds can't thrive there, even though it may look like there are miles and miles of good cover.

Let's look more closely at the four important habitats for sage grouse within the sagebrush community. Good breeding habitat means leks or strutting grounds in the form of openings or clearings surrounded by a canopy of sagebrush cover. Nesting habitat must offer concealment with a combination of sage shrub and carryover grassy cover. And this kind of cover has to be within a mile or two of the lek habitat.

Brood-rearing habitat must include insects and diverse, abundant succulent green forbs throughout the entire summer and fall, with an open canopy of sage cover. Alfalfa fields, roadside ditches, reservoirs, and other moist areas work well as long as sage cover is close by. Finally, for winter habitat, sage grouse need relatively tall expanses of sagebrush. It's important for the sage to be high enough that it doesn't get covered by snow. Snow depth is a limiting factor for good winter range. In some areas, the birds are forced to migrate long distances, or they may simply shift from a summer site to a more favorable winter site nearby.

No other North American game bird is as dependent on

Leigh Perkins swings on a big male sage grouse.

one food source as the sage grouse. Sage provides over 70 percent of the birds' year-round diet. The rest comes from succulent forbs such as dandelions, alfalfa, pussytoes, and clover. Chicks start on a full diet of animal matter like ants, beetles, and other small insects. Adult birds will eat a few insect if they become available.

Hunting Strategies

Sage grouse are our largest North American grouse. I think of them as a western trophy bird, much like a mountain sheep would be to a big game hunter, although hunting these birds doesn't require an expensive outfitted hunt. If you're planning a hunting trip for other prairie upland game birds and are in the vicinity of sage grouse territory, I highly recommend pursuing them. It's well worth the effort and it takes you into country not shared by many.

The country, like the bird, is big, wide, and handsome. The sight of twenty or thirty large black-and-white prairie bombers catapulting into the sky all at once will get your attention. Just seeing a big sage grouse airborne is a memorable experience, whether you kill one or not.

There are many square miles of sage grouse country and it's not always easy to find birds, but when you do the action can be fast and furious. Like most creatures, grouse follow a routine throughout the day. Learn their daily movements, and you will have a better chance of finding them at any given time.

Always take advantage of alfalfa fields that are in relatively close proximity to large sagebrush areas. Sage grouse love to eat legumes and will go out of their way to find them. CRP fields near sagebrush areas are also good places to find feeding birds. These rehabilitated grassland fields have many succulent dandelion and alfalfa greens.

When hunting sagebrush country early in the season, search around reservoirs, drainages, marshes, and any other low areas where succulent green plants grow. Just remember that in wet years greens will usually be available throughout the sage country, and birds will be more scattered.

Around midday, sage grouse seek out higher sagebrush under which they can loaf and rest. Sparse sagebrush areas are used for dusting. Hillsides are important for cooling off during hot weather and for warming up on cold days, depending on the time of year and the orientation of the slope.

Sage grouse don't get off the ground as quickly as most other birds, but once underway they provide excellent targets. And they typically fly much farther after the flush than other prairie game birds.

About Dogs

As with all the game birds discussed in this book, I believe sage grouse are hunted most effectively with pointing dogs. Young birds hold well for a pointing dog, and an experienced dog will have little or no problem hunting sage grouse for the first time. These birds give off a lot of scent. Sage grouse will walk, or even run, from a dog on point,

Of all the prairie grouse, sage grouse hold the best for a pointing dog.

though. So the dog may have to relocate once or twice, but the birds rarely move very far.

Sage grouse are flock birds, but they usually spread out while feeding or resting, which means that the dogs are usually pointing only one or two birds. One thing sage grouse like to do when pursued is to try to get behind or downwind of the intruder.

The birds become a little more difficult to approach later in the season. A pointing dog has to learn to be more cautious and point birds from farther away as the season progresses. And a mature flock of sage grouse can't be hunted day after day. They have good eyesight and become extremely wary if pushed.

Flushing dogs are used a lot on sage grouse because the birds live in fairly heavy cover. These dogs can plow through the brushy sage and get birds in the air quickly. They can't cover as much ground as pointing dogs because they must hunt close to be effective, but if you have identified likely areas to search before or during the hunt a flushing dog can be a real asset.

No matter what breed you use, be sure to carry water for both you and your dogs in sage grouse country because water holes are often few and far between.

It's certainly possible to hunt sage grouse without dogs, too. Concentrate your activity around reservoirs and wet areas, particularly during the early season when temperatures may still be quite high. Sage grouse will run on you, but if you stalk them quickly they will hold. Another method of hunting without dogs is to drive designated roads in sagebrush country looking for birds.

Where to Go

Sage grouse can be hunted in nine western states. At this time, Oregon, California, Colorado, Utah, and North Dakota allow hunting by permit only or have a very short season. Idaho, Nevada, Wyoming, and Montana are your best bets, as each of these states currently has good huntable populations. Sage grouse seasons change often from year to year because of population dynamics. Always check the regulations carefully when planning a trip.

For traveling wingshooters who want to take sage grouse, I usually suggest planning a combination hunt to an area that has multiple game bird species available. These are great birds to hunt, but killing one is enough. They really should be treated like trophy animals.

Snow Grouse

Sometimes the sun coming through Emit's south-facing kitchen window is so bright that I have to scoot the tractor seat chair into the shadows. But clouds hang low over the sagebrush basin this morning. It's cold for this time a year and frost clings to the sagebrush beyond the house. Emit hands me a cup of steaming black instant coffee. I thank him, still staring out the window.

"Did I ever tell you the story…" Emit begins, then knocks out his pipe, fills it with Prince Albert tobacco, sucks it to life from a wooden match, and takes a long sip of coffee "…of the time my brother and I, we were still in grade school, shot two sage chickens in the snow? It was Saturday, and our chore for the day was to pick up a load of firewood in the hills that we had cut back in the summer. Lots of snow was on the ground so we took the horse-drawn skid across the sage flats to the hills. On the way, Otto spotted a bunch of sage grouse out in the flats. Lucky for us, we had our shotguns along to maybe pot a cottontail for supper.

"We spent a half day stalking the birds in the tall sage. After getting all wet and cold, we each finally killed a bird when they flushed, the first we ever killed in the air.

"The family liked eating sage grouse. Dad or us boys would pick a young bird or two off with the .22 rifle while working cattle and Mom would fry 'em up for breakfast or lunch.

"Well, we were as proud as peacocks, so we went back to the ranch without getting the firewood to show off the two big sage grouse we'd brought for supper. Our old man got madder than a grizzly and made us clean and feather the two big roosters out in the cold. After he cooled down he said, 'Well, boys, you just don't shoot those big grouse late in the season when they're only feeding on sage. But, by golly, you're going to eat them. And tomorrow you're going to have to double up and get two loads of firewood.'

"Mom was a little better about the whole thing, but said she wouldn't fix 'em because they were two old toms and if baked they would bounce like a hard rubber ball. But she did make stew out of them the next day. It wasn't bad, thanks to all the spuds and carrots and the other stuff she put in. If I recall, the dog ate most of the meat."

After he finishes the familiar tale, which I've heard every year since I started hunting his place, Emit puts on his boots, taps the tobacco out the pipe on the edge of the stove, and gets his Carhartt coat, vest, and Winchester Model 12 pump-action shotgun. Then we both go out the door.

The frost has left the tops of the sage.

"Looks like a good day to hunt grouse, Ben. How many dogs do you have with you?"

"Four," I answer.

Like me, Emit still loves to be around these beautiful birds.

PART TWO
PLANNING THE HUNT

I'm lucky enough to live in a place that has outstanding bird hunting, but I still travel to hunt. Because no place in North America has every species of game bird in one general location, any hunter who wants the experience of hunting them all has to travel at some point. But planning efficiently and effectively to make the hunt a success often seems overwhelming. The method I detail below changes all of that.

Building a Successful Bird-Hunting Pyramid

Wherever I travel to bird hunt, my goal from beginning to end is to have fun. Planning the trip is an essential first step on the journey, and it may well be the most important building block for success. This step-by-step plan, along with all the detailed advice on where to collect information, will make the process easy and enjoyable.

A successful bird-hunting pyramid starts with a solid foundation. Each level has to be in place before you can continue moving toward your goal at the top. The challenge lies in narrowing your choices for building blocks and in making good decisions level by level. It's really quite simple, but to get the best results the pyramid has to be built from the bottom up.

The Pyramid	Birds

The Pyramid

Birds

Being There

Equipment • What to Bring

Getting There • Accommodations

Locations • Maps • Atlas • Gazetteer • Books

Public or Private Lands •Agency Listings • Dogs or Not

Bird Distribution • Select the Bird to Hunt • Select the States

The Right Approach to Gathering Info • Web • Write •E-mail •Call

How to Gather Information

Knowing how to collect the right information is the first tool for building a strong foundation in your bird hunting pyramid. Start by collecting general information on where to hunt the bird you've chosen. Acquire information packets from the states that interest you. Surf the Internet, send an e-mail, write a letter, or call the specific fish and game agencies.

The material will include general information about bird hunting and regulations. It won't contain current information about bird numbers, population counts, habitat conditions, and the best areas to hunt. Your next step is to compile a list of questions that you can refer to later when talking to knowledgeable personnel in the fish and game agencies.

Using the Internet

Many hunters are now Internet-savvy. But even if you haven't used the Web to search for information before, it's not difficult to master. Start by asking for help from family members or friends. Using the Internet is now the fastest way to collect preliminary information about bird hunting from state agencies.

The Web is also a wonderful tool for gathering pertinent travel information. Any one of the many search engines will lead you to a wealth of great resources for every aspect of trip planning.

Writing a Letter or E-mail

Remember that when writing or e-mailing at this stage you are simply gathering information, not looking for a specific place to hunt. Be sure to make this clear in your introduction, and briefly list the exact information you want. Busy people in the outdoor information field are often barraged with questions, so the chances of getting a personal letter back are remote. Most of the information you receive will be general printed material.

You can also acquire this general information by calling the state fish and game agencies. You'll usually be talking to a low-level employee at this point, so just ask for their standard information packet for bird hunters. Even if hunting information for the upcoming season is not in print yet, ask for last year's packet. And get on their mailing list so you can receive the new information when it's ready. Season dates are usually fairly similar year to year.

Review this information and prepare your questions before trying to contact higher-level agency personnel for more specific information pertaining to your target species.

Using the General Information

The general information you collect from each state should give you a solid foundation for compiling pertinent questions for your more specific phone conversations.

Here are some things to consider:

1. Contact information for region or area offices or specific biologist.
2. State programs that provide access to private lands.
3. Publications for public lands to hunt, such as walk-in and sign-up areas.
4. State lands and refuges that allow hunting.
5. Helpful publications available for bird hunters, whether free or for a fee.
6. State maps available for bird hunting, whether free or for a fee.
7. Federal lands to hunt within the state borders.
8. The best time to call back about game bird population trends.
10. The general climate and typical weather changes throughout the hunting season.
11. The best time to hunt the specific species you've chosen.
12. The kind of habitat in which the birds live.
13. Inform them that you have a dog.
14. Ask any personal questions that may help you (e.g., Is it hard walking?).

After compiling the list, call the game agencies of the states that interest you. Always try to get through to an information specialist or, better yet, a game biologist, if available. These people are knowledgeable about their state's resources and can give you an excellent overview of the hunting there.

Get the names and phone numbers of the regional biologists in the locations within the state that you plan to hunt. If a biologist isn't available in that area, ask for the game warden's phone number. And don't be afraid to ask to talk to these people. It's part of their job, so be courteous but persistent. If you are prepared for the calls and are frank and friendly, you'll often be pleasantly surprised by all the great information you receive.

The Right Approach to Calling

The reason for calling higher-level information officers and wildlife biologists is to collect current and specific information that will eventually help you determine the best place to hunt. So these phone calls are extremely important.

In my opinion, there's a right way and a wrong way to go about gathering this type of information, no matter whom you're talking to. Remember, the person on the other end of the line is usually busy with other work, so don't just ramble on. Use the list you prepared so that you can get the pertinent information you need quickly.

Be courteous, friendly, and direct. Give the person your name and briefly explain why you're calling. Be specific with your questions. Have a notebook and pencil handy, along with maps of the state or area you're inquiring about. Take

Making a Call

The best approach could be something like: "Hello, my name is John Smith. I live in Iowa, and I'm interested in hunting sharp-tailed grouse. I'm looking for information, and was wondering if I could ask you a few questions to help me locate some good general areas to hunt birds."

Then have suitable questions ready for the expert you're talking to. Don't just ask where the best places to hunt birds are in the state. That rarely nets a good answer. Instead, make sure it sounds like you've done your homework and that you're looking for help in finding a good starting point. Tell them you will call again when hunting season draws near.

notes as you listen, and make sure to get the numbers of other information officers or biologists that work in the areas you are thinking about hunting.

Select the Bird You Plan to Hunt

I know there are a few devoted hunters who focus solely on one kind of game bird, but most wingshooters like traveling to new places to seek different species. Some regions have more than one species of game bird available. Just remember that when planning a trip it's better to keep the initial focus on a single species. Later on, you can consider secondary species, but don't let them get in the way of your main objective.

Selecting States or Provinces

At this stage, it's important to select several states because you don't know where the best hunting is yet. Part One of this book offers an overview of states or provinces that traditionally offer good hunting for prairie birds, but bird populations are fluid and may change significantly from year to year. Search for states that have a reliable record of good bird hunting on public and private lands that are open to the average hunter.

Use the same approach when collecting information from provincial agencies. Call for current information on the upcoming hunting season. Ask about crown (public) lands, the policy for hunting private holdings, and about other agencies and information that may help a traveling wingshooter. The Canadian provinces are usually good about sending up-to-date hunting information, maps, travel publications, and the names of other agencies involved with bird hunting.

Planning a Trip Using Population Densities

For prairie game birds, population densities change periodically throughout the bird's range because of different land-use practices, agricultural improvements, and other factors that are detrimental to habitat. So population levels can decline or increase over a long or short period of time in some areas.

Numbers also fluctuate because of seasonal weather conditions. And weather plays an important part in determining local population numbers within a specific area. It's possible to find good hunting in one region of the state or province and poor bird numbers in another region.

Information from wildlife agencies will help you make the initial decision about which state or province to hunt. First, it's important to get positive long-term population counts in several areas you are considering. By doing this, you can key into areas that have had good numbers of birds in the past, although it is essential to follow up later when more data becomes available from biologists and other wildlife personal in the field.

Because sharptails, sage grouse, and prairie chicken gather on breeding grounds in the spring, it's relatively easy for field biologists to collect data on yearly bird numbers in a given area. These numbers are then used to project the density of birds in that area for the fall hunting season. Getting this information is important and should help you finalize the location you plan to hunt.

Getting solid information on Huns is a little more difficult because the birds pair up in the spring instead of gathering on leks. Very little information about population trends is available early on, but as late summer approaches, young Hun coveys become much more visible along gravel roads and other open areas. This gives field biologists and other field researchers a chance to put together some projections for the fall.

Call Federal Agencies

Next, call all the federal agencies that oversee public lands in the states you've selected. Ask to speak with the game biologists or information officers within these departments—national wildlife refuges, the Forest Service (national forests or grasslands), the Bureau of Land Management, and tribal reservations. Refer back to your list of questions when calling these agencies. For Canada, call the national agencies listed in the hunter's information packet that you received.

Choosing Locations to Hunt

Begin to focus on locations within the states or provinces you are considering about six months in advance of the tentative timeframe for your hunt. The final selection of where to hunt can only come from reviewing the current, accurate information about bird populations that you'll get as the season approaches. Department biologists working in the field collect this information, and it usually isn't available until a few months before hunting season.

If bird populations have declined, adjust your plans so

Licenses

In many states it's possible to purchase a hunting licenses over the phone, on the Internet, or by writing. In other states, it's just as easy to buy the license after you arrive. Each state has it's own licensing agenda for nonresidents.

Be aware of license fees, seasonal dates for each game bird, possession limits, land-use regulations, and other information pertinent to the bird hunter. Make sure you acquire all this information before you decide which state to hunt. Make it a point to completely read the hunting regulations.

that you're hunting where the birds are, not where they used to be. Be prepared to change locations.

Make a new list of questions to ask regional information officers or biologists that includes the following:

1. Past population trends.
2. Population trends for the coming year, if any.
3. Call counts in the spring.
4. Weather trends during winter, spring, summer that may have affected this year's bird population.
5. Cover type—at the time of the call and during the hunting season.
6. Best times to hunt.
7. Private and public lands available to hunt in the area.
8. The names of businesses and sporting goods stores in the area that cater to hunters.
9. Add a few of your own questions, maybe something about any fee-hunting possibilities or local people that may be helpful with hunting information.

Start contacting personnel that deal directly with game bird management. You should now be finished talking to the experts in the main office or headquarters. It's time to branch out and talk to the regional information officers or biologists, which will allow you to take advantage of accurate, specific information on population trends and densities. Talk to anyone with hands-on duties in the field, or at least someone who has regular contact with those in the field. This is when you'll really begin zeroing in on a place to hunt.

Ask for current information about bird numbers, population counts, habitat conditions, and the best general areas to hunt. And check on public and private land. If you ask a few questions in a polite manner, most of the information will flow freely.

Ask for the names of local businesses that carter to bird hunters or other folks that could be of help. If this nets any local contacts, follow up with them immediately. This could be a sporting goods store, motel, or other local business.

Once you have as much of this information as you can gather, decide on the best state or province. But still consider several locations within that state or province. Set hunting dates to coincide with the most favorable weather conditions in that region.

As the trip draws near, call the most reliable contacts you previously made for the latest information. Then make the final decision about which state or province to hunt.

Locating Land to Hunt Before You Go to Public Lands

Some of the best hunting for many of our North American game birds can be had on public lands. Western and upper Midwestern states have thousands and thousands of acres of public land available. Many states actually have more public lands than they do private holdings. Maps from federal agencies will help you identify public lands, and the DeLorme Atlas & Gazetteers and the Benchmark Map books are also helpful.

Private Lands

Many state wildlife agencies have established cooperative agreements with private landowners to provide free public hunting on private property and on isolated public land. For example, Montana has a very successful Block Management Program and South Dakota has what it calls Walk-In Areas. Many other states now have, or are planning, such programs. Always ask about these programs; they are a wonderful aid in finding land to hunt.

Many local chambers of commerce can be helpful in finding private places for traveling wingshooters to hunt. They are also good about sending brochures that advertise local businesses, and they usually have maps of the surrounding area. Local motels and sporting goods stores may also help you find private lands to hunt. All of these businesses are interested in bringing hunting dollars into their community.

Some communities even provide a list of local farmers or ranchers who allow hunting. Some of these might ask a small trespass fee, but in most cases you receive good value for your money. This may even lead you to other private places to hunt.

Another way to find good hunting ground is through word of mouth from friends and acquaintances that may have hunted the location you plan to visit. Make some calls to folks you know who have hunted these places in past years. Call local newspaper and magazine columnists for information about where to hunt. I get a lot of phone calls like this each year, which is one of the reasons I'm writing

On hot days a dog needs to cool down.

this book. I want to make it easier for the traveling wing-shooter to find a good place to hunt.

Many county seats have plat maps available that show private land ownership. This is public information. Once you have a chance to hunt or look over a specific area, identify likely bird hunting country and then check the plat maps. Don't call them; instead, visit the owner face-to-face at a reasonable time of day. Timing is extremely important. Never go too early in the morning or late in the evening.

When you first meet the landowner, whether he or she is working outside or at home, introduce yourself. Tell them where you live and what you do. If you have a bird dog, mention it. Most farmers and ranchers like dogs and respect people who have animals. Tell them you are hunting in the area for a few days, then ask if it's possible to hunt birds on their place. Be very polite no matter what the answer is.

Courtesy and an open, friendly attitude will get you everywhere. If they refuse you, thank them for their time anyway. You'll be surprised how helpful they can be in suggesting neighbors that allow hunting or public lands you may not know about

Bureau of Indian Affairs, Tribal Lands

A large percentage of Native Americans still live on reservations. But not all tribal lands permit hunting. After you select a location, the state wildlife agency can help you locate open tribal lands. In most cases, the best idea is to call the individual reservation directly for hunting information, because each usually has its own regulations. The DeLorme Atlas & Gazetteers and the Benchmark Maps usually list tribal recreational lands.

Tribal lands that are open to hunting require permit fees. In some places, both a state and tribal fee may be necessary. Other states don't force you to purchase a state license if you're hunting on tribal lands.

Canadian Provinces

Canadian provinces have rural municipality maps showing land ownership. Grid maps are also available, and these are very useful in finding your way around. My experience has been that most Canadians are very hospitable about letting

Firearms in Canada

Canada has strict laws about firearms. Since these are federal laws, they apply throughout the country. If you're planning a bird-hunting trip over the border you'll need to gather information about registering your guns with Canada Customs. You also must declare your firearms with U.S. Customs prior to leaving the U.S. This can be done at most U.S. airports or at the border crossing prior to going into Canada. (This declaration serves as proof of ownership when entering Canada.)

A hunter entering Canada is required to fill out a Non-Restricted Firearms Declaration, Form JUS 909. These forms are available from the Canada Firearms Center by calling 1-800-731-4000 (if you live in the U.S.) or 506-624-5380 (if you live elsewhere) or via their website at www.cfc.gc.ca.

To save time, it's recommended that this triplicate form be filled out prior to the trip. Just make sure you leave the signature block blank, because it must be signed in the presence of a Canadian Customs officer at the border. When signing, some form of photo identification is required. The cost of this declaration is currently $50.00 (Canadian).

For additional information on the declaration process you can also call the Canada Customs and Revenue Agency at 204-983-3500 or 506-636-5064.

The hassle of going through this process is not as bad as it seems, and hunting prairie birds in the provinces of Canada is a true delight.

folks hunt their land. Canada also has thousands of acres of crown (public) lands and wildlife areas to hunt.

Check with each province for regulations about hunting

private lands. The land in some provinces may be open to hunting if not posted; not so in others. Each province will send you a complete packet of information that covers all hunting regulations.

Make sure you check with Canadian authorities about bringing guns and other hunting equipment across the border before finalizing your trip. Once you arrive in Canada you can travel from province to province just as we do from state to state without being checked for hunting gear. Even with all the border regulations on both sides, the Canadian provinces are a great place to hunt upland game birds.

Keep in mind that each province has its own rules for hunting. So be aware of their nonresident regulations, as some provinces have areas that are closed to nonresident hunters. And they may have reduced bag and possession limits for nonresidents. Make sure you understand all of the bird hunting regulations in the province before heading out.

MAP SOURCES
Commercial Maps

As a traveling bird hunter, some of the best maps you can own are the DeLorme Atlas & Gazetteers and/or the Benchmark Road and Recreation Atlases for the states you're considering. These maps have various scales from about 1:250,000 (1 inch represents 4 miles) to 1:500,000 (1 inch represents 8 miles).

These large paperback books contain quadrangular maps that cover the entire state, and they're helpful for locating general areas you plan to hunt and for figuring out driving routes. They are also a great resource to have at hand when talking to personnel at federal and state agencies.

They make it easy to find public lands and identify private holdings. Both series have full-color maps that clearly show state and federal lands. The maps also list all the recreation sites, facilities, and outdoor activities available in the state. These map books even list contact information for the Bureau of Land Management, U.S. Forest Service, U.S. Fish and Wildlife Service, Army Corps of Engineers, Bureau of Indian Affairs, Department of Tourism, and regional fish and game offices.

I don't go anywhere without them.

The DeLorme Atlas & Gazetteers are available for all fifty states. At this time, the Benchmark Atlases are available for California, Oregon, Washington, Arizona, New Mexico, Utah, Nevada, and Idaho. They cost about twenty to twenty-five dollars each and are well worth it. Both big map books are widely available at retailers or online.

Public Maps

By now, you should have acquired a state highway map and the hunting regulations maps. State highway maps are available from the tourism departments in each state. Some states include this map with their hunting regulations.

States like Oklahoma have even compiled large atlases of public lands open to hunting. These map books are outstanding, and they're worth every penny.

Many states have state forests and state trust lands. Contact the appropriate state wildlife agency to obtain maps of these areas, which are usually open to hunting

BLM Maps

The Bureau of Land Management (BLM), an agency within the Department of the Interior, administers 261 million acres of America's public lands, located primarily in twelve western states. They produce the best maps for precisely locating private and public lands, indexed by quadrangles. These maps are also helpful in determining access to public lands.

These are topographic maps, also known as surface management maps, and have a scale of 1:100,000 (1 centimeter represents 1 kilometer; that's about 1 inch for every 1.58 miles). The maps are detailed and color-coded for public and private lands. They also show topographical features.

You can call, write, or go online to order these maps, and it's often best to start by obtaining an index map (free of charge) that shows what individual maps are available for the state. And BLM personnel can usually help you figure out which maps you need right over the phone if you know the county you're planning to visit. These maps cost around five dollars.

Forest Service Maps

The U.S. Forest Service administers millions of acres of public land in America's national forests and grasslands. They produce maps for each of these areas. The scale for most maps is 1:126,720 (1/2 inch represents 1 mile). These are excellent maps, and they usually show miles of the surrounding area. They are detailed and color-coded for federal, state, and private land. They also show township and section-line classifications and include the index to geological survey topographic maps. These maps are reasonably priced at around five to ten dollars each.

USGS Maps

Topographic maps from the United States Geological Survey (USGS) provide even more detail than BLM maps. These maps are on a scale of 1:24,000 (2 1/2 inches represents 1 mile). Now that's detail! These maps are often overkill for hunting upland game birds in open areas, but they come in handy in mountainous or heavily wooded country.

Getting the right maps can be tricky because they cover such a small area. Before you order a specific map, you'll need to request a catalog and index of the state you're interested in. Some sporting goods stores carry USGS maps of the areas around them.

U.S. Fish and Wildlife Service Maps

There are more than 475 national wildlife refuges in the U.S., at least one in every state. These cover 91 million acres and protect nearly every kind of wild animal native to the continent. Many of refuges allow limited upland bird hunting, and hunting can be excellent at times. After you select the state you plan to hunt, contact the fish and game agency and ask if any national wildlife refuges offer bird hunting. All refuges are listed with each state wildlife agency.

U.S. Army Corps of Engineers Maps

Many federal Army Corps of Engineers lands are listed and/or managed by state and other national agencies. The DeLorme Atlas & Gazetteers and the Benchmark Atlases show Army Corps of Engineers recreational lands.

Accommodations and Getting There

There are two general categories for accommodations: stationary and mobile. Stationary arrangements include renting a house, staying with a friend, or, most likely, staying in a motel or hotel. Mobile accommodations include pulling a trailer, taking a pickup camper or RV, or roughing it in a tent. Each type has advantages and disadvantages.

Camping

National, state, and private campgrounds offer good cheap places to stay. On many federal lands, you can camp almost anywhere. Camping is obviously cost efficient, and being on or near your prospective hunting grounds can make for a very good hunt because you spend less time in transit and more time afield. There's nothing like getting far away from everyone else when hunting certain birds. Like any other game, birds react unfavorably to a great deal of hunting pressure, and camping can give you an edge over hunters who must hunt closer to the city or town where they're staying.

The obvious disadvantage to camping lies in having less basic comforts available. You can't come in from a hard day of hunting and relax in great style.

Getting information about camping is quite simple. All the federal agencies and state and provincial departments mentioned previously have information about campgrounds and camping rules. For public camping in individual states, write or call chambers of commerce, tourism offices, and fish and game departments. The DeLorme Atlas & Gazetteers and the Benchmark Map books also show campgrounds. The Internet is another great place to find camping information.

Moteling It

Most folks who travel to hunt birds choose a small-town motel or hotel for their accommodations. These facilities are the easiest to find, and many cater to hunters and their dogs. After a long day, there's nothing like a hot shower, a good meal at a cafe or restaurant, and a decent bed to sleep in. And a hard-hunting dog appreciates these comforts, as well. But staying in town often means a long drive to your hunting grounds, although if the bird hunting turns out to be poor, you have the flexibility to quickly relocate to another town.

Getting information about staying in a motel is mostly a matter of making a phone call or two. State tourism offices and local and county chambers of commerce are excellent resources for accommodations.

There are many motel chains. One example is Best

Western (1-800-WESTERN), which produces traveler's guides that list all their motels, services, and whether or not dogs are allowed. If you're a member, the American Automobile Association (AAA) has tour books that list motels, restaurants, local chambers of commerce, recreation opportunities, and much more for each state. Also, using the Internet is an easy way to find accommodations throughout the United States and Canada. It's always nice to have a place to stay locked in before you leave home.

Driving

The smooth highways that crisscross America and the comfort of modern vehicles make driving a pleasure these days. Driving not only can make for a good hunting trip, it can also make for a good scenic vacation. No matter where you're going, allow yourself ample driving time so you aren't exhausted when you arrive. Driving to the place you plan to hunt can also give your body more time to adjust to things like time zone changes and higher altitudes.

My preference is always to drive if at all possible. Nothing beats having your own hunting rig along, with all of your gear stowed in its normal place. I can take as many guns as I like, and since I have lots of hunting dogs I can carry as many as I see fit. Also, driving allows you to hunt other places along the way to your final destination. But the biggest advantages are mobility and the ability to change plans quickly based on prevailing conditions.

Flying

Most hunters drive to good bird country, but sometimes flying is easier. It all depends on how far your destination is, the amount of gear you have to haul, and if you're traveling with dogs. Flying has some definite advantages. If you have limited time and must travel a long distance, this may be your only option. When I bird hunt in Alaska, I go by air. Even from Montana, Alaska represents four days of driving—each way. Although if you have a full month in which to hunt, driving would be well worth the time.

You'd be surprised at how close you can get to good bird country by flying. The place you select to hunt should be less than a half-day's drive from an airport. The downside of traveling by air is that you are restricted to a central location. If the bird hunting doesn't live up to your expectations, moving a significant distance is out of the question.

Flying does take a little more planning than driving. Make sure you can rent an off-road vehicle. Bird hunting is a rural sport, and no matter what species you hunt, gravel and dirt roads usually lead to the best areas. Also, when traveling by air, the amount of hunting gear you can bring is limited. And taking a dog or two is an added expense.

Airlines today have strict regulations on shipping firearms, ammunition, and gear. Many airlines allow only two checked pieces of luggage with a maximum of fifty pounds each. They may charge you extra for anything over that.

A security agent will ask you to open up your gun case. Make sure you take a roll of duct tape, and use it to tape the case shut after the inspection so it doesn't pop open in transit. If you're carrying ammunition make sure it's stored separately from the gun.

Each airline has different rules for carrying dogs. Weather conditions, such as extreme cold or hot temperatures, may prevent you from taking your dog along. In fact, airlines can refuse a dog on any flight at any time, whether you are heading out to hunt or coming home.

Before you book a flight, make sure you have all the details from the airline's customer service department related to the amount of luggage, weight limits, transporting guns, ammo storage, coolers for taking game birds home, canine requirements, and check-in times.

Hunting Dogs

Today, the majority of upland gunners have a hunting dog or two, and the traveling hunter is more likely to have dog than not. Traveling with a dog is quite different from going alone, particularly as most bird dogs these days are also family pets.

Wingshooting Wisdom is not about finding the perfect breed of dog to hunt each prairie game bird. It's about finding the best hunting opportunities, no matter what dogs you take afield.

Traveling With a Hunting Dog

Hunting without a dog means you can travel as you would on any other vacation. You can drive for hours, stop at any motel, and have meals whenever you want. You can take side trips and leave the vehicle unattended for hours. But traveling with a dog changes everything.

The more dogs one has, the more complicated traveling becomes. My hunting rig is equipped to carry eight to twelve dogs, depending on the breed. I have a custom-designed fiberglass canine carrier mounted on the bed of my

Traveling with a dog is quite different from going alone.

pickup. I've used the same carrier for almost thirty years and have modified it to fit six different pickups. One thing's for sure, it has hauled a lot of different dogs across much of the country. And it has been economical, durable, and safe and comfortable for the dogs.

My friend Tom Davis uses an aluminum dog trailer to carry his setters when traveling. Just like me, Tom makes sure his dogs are well cared for before anything else.

If you have only one dog, a good carrier is still essential. A standard air cargo dog crate is fine, and this is how most bird dogs are transported today. Make sure the crate is roomy enough, has a flat and comfortable surface and good ventilation away from exhaust fumes, and is securely fastened so it doesn't slide around when the vehicle is moving.

Traveling with dogs takes a little extra planning. Here are a few ideas I use that may be helpful, even if you have only one dog. First, start with a consistent routine. While traveling, I keep my dogs on the same daily schedule they're used to. Feeding times at home are eight o'clock in the morning and again at five in the evening. Even if I change time zones, I stay on the old schedule until I arrive at my destination.

I take the dogs' everyday food and water pans. These are made of stainless steel and stack together, which makes them easy to transport. I pack several white square plastic buckets of dog food. Taking water from home is also a good idea, although most drinking water throughout North America is safe. Changing to different water when traveling is not a big issue with me, as long as it comes from a bottle or clean tap. When exercising your dogs during the trip, give them a drink of fresh water from their own clean watering pan. Don't let the dogs drink open, standing water that appears foul or stagnant. Bad water can give a dog diarrhea, so I stay away from runoff water, puddles, and other water that may be contaminated.

I always feed the dogs at the same time, with the same pans, the same food, and in the same amounts. If a dog refuses to eat when traveling I simply take the food away. Routine makes for a happy dog. They eat, rest, sleep, drink, exercise, and clean out at the same times they do at home. Believe me, this works great and saves a lot of hassle.

Besides my kennel dogs, I keep a couple of hunting house dogs, but they have the same routine as all the other dogs. Being house pets, I prefer to have them in the motel room, but I never leave them unattended. For safety reasons, I don't padlock the dog compartments on the truck when on the road, although I do when the vehicle is stationary.

Look for a motel before sunset. The ideal motel will have parking available in front of the room, with easy access. I prefer a motel that has a large field adjacent to it or a good exercise area close by, like a park or a recreation area. After checking in, I go directly to the exercise area. I release two to four dogs at a time, depending on how secure the area is. A pan of water is always available for the dogs during their exercise period.

Back at the motel, the dogs are fed in their kennel compartments before I tend to myself. And before retiring for the night I exercise the dogs again. I follow the same routine at first light; the dogs are fed their morning meal before I go to breakfast. Once on the road, the dogs are exercised around ten o'clock and again in early afternoon a couple of hours before I plan to arrive at the next motel. When traveling, exercising a dog twice a day is plenty.

I try to avoid public rest stops for exercising the dogs, as there's usually too much traffic, too many distractions, and too many other canine smells. Instead, I look for frontage roads that parallel the interstate or highway, preferably gravel roads that aren't used much. Many of these roads have woven-wire fencing on both sides, making them excel-

Keep all your hunting gear together; that way nothing is left behind.

lent places to safely exercise more than one dog at a time. Gravel pits, abandoned railroad tracks, state and federal lands, and traffic-free open areas are all good places to exercise dogs on the road.

After traveling the same routes year after year, I know where the dog-friendly motels are and have pinned down the good exercise locations.

Packing

Your specific travel plans will dictate what you need to take on a bird-hunting trip. The amount of time spent on the road and actually hunting, the climate, time of year, and type of travel all have to be considered. Traveling with a hunting partner and dogs also changes the scope of what to bring. So every packing situation is different because no travel plan is the same. Still, I'm sure we all go through the same thing: What do I really need?

Knowing the overall climate and general weather patterns for the time of your hunt will help you figure out what clothes to pack. So get up-to-the-minute weather information and the long-range forecast for your destination. Today's forecasts are quite accurate, and it's well worth the time to check them out. Watching the Weather Channel on television, logging onto the Internet, reading the newspaper, and listening to the radio are all good ways to learn what the long-range forecasts are for the area you plan to hunt.

Packing for Travel

One nice thing about driving your own rig is that you'll have all your gear ready to go at the drop of a hat, so packing really isn't a problem. But you should still write down a list of all the equipment you have with you before departing from home.

Flying takes a little extra planning because weight becomes an important element. You can take almost the same gear when flying commercially as when driving, but there are exceptions, such as aerosol cans, matches, and other combustible items. Contact the airline and ask what items are restricted for travel.

If you'll be taking a dog with you, check with the airlines

for their animal policies and restrictions. One bit of advice: Airline personnel are usually unfamiliar of hunting dog paraphernalia. So if you're taking an electronic collar or beeper collar, remove the batteries before packing them. I once had a beeper collar sound off in my luggage after I checked in at the airport terminal. Lucky for me, it happened many years ago, before all the new security restrictions were in place.

You probably won't need most of the items that are restricted. My strategy is to take only the minimum amount of inner and outer clothing necessary. Hunting clothing is now much lighter, more compact, and warmer than in years past. Choose lightweight, durable clothing, but don't sacrifice quality.

Boots are a different story, even when flying. Bird hunting is a walking sport, so good broken-in hunting boots are a necessity. I bring at least two pairs of good strong walking boots, with at least one waterproof pair.

Dress Wear

My dress code strategy for days afield near home or far away is to always dress for walking and to keep clothing loose for good movement.

Don't wear too many layers over your arms, as this hampers your ability to shoulder the gun properly. I use a warm vest when it's cold, which leaves my arms free, I wear synthetic stretch clothing underneath.

Most hunting trousers are made for comfort or protection, but few possess both qualities. I like light, strong pants for hunting open country in warm weather, and tough, lightweight, briar-resistant trousers for cold weather and heavy cover. But either style must fit loosely and provide comfortable movement when climbing hills or stepping high. Loose trousers are also cooler in warm weather. During cold weather, I wear a pair of synthetic long johns underneath. The light, form-fitting, stretchy material still allows me good movement when walking.

Pant lengths should be on the short side, about a third of the way up the boot or three inches above the ground. Pants cut short and without cuffs may not be fashionable, but they're cooler, stay cleaner, and allow you to walk through cover more easily. I use the same trousers for wet or snowy weather, although I often slip on lightweight, water-proof chaps or bibs.

Upland bird hunting almost always requires a lot of walking, so proper foot care is essential. Footwear can make or break a hunting trip, and to me it's the most important element of the outfit. Good boots cost some money, but they'll last a lot longer than a cheap pair. It's usually best to try boots on before buying them, although I've had good luck buying boots from mail-order catalogs, many of which have a bigger selection with more brands than you can find locally. If you do buy boots through the mail, don't hesitate to exchange or return them if the fit is uncomfortable. You'll be thankful in the long run.

I like hunting boots with moccasin-style toes. Other folks

may find the round toes more comfortable. Whatever the case, find a good brand that fits well and then stick with them. And there's no such thing as an all-purpose hunting boot; one pair of boots doesn't cut it for all hunting conditions.

My cold-weather hunting boots are full leather, insulated, and Gore-Tex. My warm-weather boots are full leather, as well, with a height of at least twelve inches and a hard lug sole for walking in all kinds of terrain. If properly oiled and resoled occasionally, both pairs of boots will last a lifetime. I haven't had much luck with ultra-light boots. I'd rather have a tougher boot with a bit more weight to clomp around in, one that gives my calves, ankles, and arches good support.

Breaking in a pair of boots is vital, so buy them long before hunting season starts. I wear new boots around the house for short intervals to get them ready for days afield.

One last bit of advice on boots: Think about using boot dryers, portable or stationary. I own both types, and the portable model is part of my traveling gear. I use boot dryers on sweaty or wet boots after each day of hunting. It's like having an extra pair of boots—but a lot cheaper.

I'm a firm believer in wearing two pairs of socks. Whenever movement occurs, the two socks rub slightly against each other, which is easier on the skin. This helps prevent blisters and absorbs additional moisture.

Hats are a matter of choice. A hat should provide protection for the entire face, but its primary function is to shade the eyes and protect the ears in cold weather.

Baseball-style hats are designed for cold or warm weather, and most are adjustable. I always insist on brightly colored hats when hunting with other folks, especially young, inexperienced hunters I don't know well.

Choosing a Shotgun

The kind of shotgun you hunt with, its gauge, and even how it's choked are all personal choices that will depend on the type of shooting you intend to do, the targeted game bird, and how much money you wish to spend. If you pursue many different species of birds, along with other shooting activities, more than one shotgun may be in order. No one shotgun can fit every shooting occasion.

To become a good shot, your gun must fit properly, and it takes practice to become reasonably skilled. The best way to keep your shooting skills honed is to shoot clay targets in the off-season. Planning also includes practicing before the trip. It may mean the difference between bringing home birds and coming back empty-handed.

But successful upland bird hunting requires more than just shooting. It also requires some knowledge of bird habits and habitat. Knowing what the birds are likely to do during and after the flush is invaluable. And the only way you can learn to shoot a particular species of game bird is through experience. Fully understanding any sport makes it easier and more enjoyable.

Because of all the walking involved, your shotgun should be fairly light. But the weight of the gun also depends on the size of the person carrying it. Flushing game birds don't give you much time to react, so a well-balanced gun is important for getting on target quickly. In general, the smaller and faster the game bird is, the lighter and quicker the shotgun should be.

Choosing a Gauge and Choke

Major shotgun gauges include the 12, 16, 20, 28, and .410. The gauge of a shotgun (other than the .410, which is a caliber size) is determined by the number of lead balls, each fitting the barrel exactly, that add up to one pound.

The 12-gauge remains the standard choice for most North American bird hunters. The 20-gauge is the next most popular, closely followed by the 28 and 16. Sporting clays have contributed to the revival in popularity of the lesser-used gauges. Due to its lack of power, the .410 isn't a good choice for prairie birds.

The amount of choke determines the effective range of the shotgun on different types of game. The choke is classified according to the percentage of pellets that strike within a thirty-inch circle at forty yards. The exception is the .410, which is patterned at thirty yards.

The three most common chokes are full, modified, and improved cylinder. If the shotgun patterns 70 percent or more at the range specified above it's a full choke. The effective range of a full choke is thirty-five to fifty-five yards, depending on the game bird and shot size. A modified choke patterns around 50 to 60 percent, and its effective

Shotguns

Many types of shotgun are available, and all have their place in the upland arena. Side-by-side double-barreled shotguns come with boxlock or sidelock actions, both of which have a long tradition in bird hunting. Double-barreled shotguns also come in an over/under configuration. These types of double-barreled shotguns dominate the sporting scene for some upland game birds.

Pump-action and semiautomatic shotguns are also popular throughout North America. Many bird hunters prefer them because of the number of shells they hold.

So take your pick. The most important thing is to become proficient with whatever shotgun you select.

range is usually twenty-five to fifty yards. If the pattern is roughly 45 to 50 percent it's an improved cylinder, with an effective range of just twenty to thirty yards.

Other chokes are useful in certain situations, as well. A cylinder bore patterns at about 30 to 40 percent. Skeet No. 1 is a little above cylinder bore. And Skeet No. 2 varies between improved cylinder and modified.

Many shotguns now come with interchangeable choke tubes, and most existing guns can be retrofitted with tubes. So it's possible for one gun to provide the hunter with chokes for a variety of game birds and conditions.

Shot Size

Recommending a specific shot size, velocity, and shot load is an easy way to launch a loud debate among upland bird hunters. The important thing to remember is that killing power lies in the amount of shot put in a given place. The larger the shot, the better it retains its velocity and range. Smaller shot sizes create denser patterns, but they don't carry as far. Generally, the best shot size for upland game birds is the smallest size that allows sufficient penetration. The more shot that hits a game bird, the greater the chance of hitting a vital area.

Does a shotgun with a thirty-inch barrel shoot farther than one with a twenty-six-inch barrel using the same load? The answer is yes—but only by four inches.

For what it's worth, here is what I recommend.

SPECIES	SHOT SIZE
Sharp-tailed Grouse	#7½ early season
	#6 late season
Prairie Chicken	#7½ early season
	#6 late season
Sage Grouse	#6 or #5 all season
Gray Partridge	#7½ early season
	#7½ or #6 late season

Other Hunting Gear

It's a good idea to wear a blaze-orange coat and vest when hunting, and many states require it during part or all of the season. Coats are for late season and cold weather; keep them loose and light.

What should you carry in a vest? Basically, just shotgun shells. The rest of the space is for carrying dead birds. And keep it light, with lots of good movement.

Every hunter should wear shooting glasses for protection. When traveling to hunt, glasses are second on my list of most important items, right behind hunting boots. For whatever reason, I seem to shoot better when wearing glasses. I prefer orange lenses because they collect light and improve object definition (e.g., a dark bird flying against a dark background).

I almost always wear shooting gloves, even in warm weather. I keep them thin and light, except in cold weather, when I switch to lightweight, Gore-Tex gloves.

I consider dog supplies as important as my personal hunting gear. I never go afield without a lanyard. It holds two whistles, a pair of long hemostats for removing thorns and porcupine quills, a comb, and small scissors for removing burrs and other unfriendly things that get into dog fur.

A complete dog first-aid kit should be close at hand at all times. Other important items include beeper collars, e-collars, leads, dog boots, pad toughener, water bottle, toenail clippers, and your dogs' health records.

Being There

It should go without saying that you need to be in good physical condition before a hunting trip. Start walking several miles a day, four or five times a week for a month before your trip. It doesn't have to be strenuous, although it needs to be active enough that you feel some improvement as time goes on. Be aware of elevation changes where you plan to hunt. A big change in elevation can affect your breathing during the first couple of days of hunting. Get plenty of sleep at night during your hunting endeavors. And drink plenty of water before, during, and after the hunt.

Being in good upland bird country is what it's all about. It's your reward for the time you spent planning the trip. Once you reach good hunting grounds, take some time to look over the whole area. No matter where you go, drive back roads and look for potential cover. It's well worth the time, and it will pay big dividends on future hunts to the region.

Take your time and talk to folks that live in the area. This could be at a local cafe, general store, sporting goods store, gas station, farm, or ranch. Kicking a little dirt with local folks can open doors to outstanding hunting on public and private lands no matter what part of North America you're visiting.

With a Dog

I certainly hope that any dog you take on a hunting trip is in good physical condition and able to hunt safely and effectively for the number of days you have planned. The best performing dogs are those at the top of their game. Dogs need off-season conditioning just like hunters do.

It's a good idea to give your dog a bit more food on a

hunting trip if he's working particularly hard. And like people, hard-working dogs should get lots of rest. Have ample water available for your dog when in the field. Water is the key to keeping a dog running hard, and it helps scenting ability. Make sure you have a warm, comfortable place for your dog to rest a night, too.

On the road or in the field, care of your dog comes first.

Caring for Game Birds

All game birds make delicious eating if taken care of properly. Some hunters like to hang or refrigerate the birds for several days before cooking them, others prefer to cook or freeze birds as quickly as possible. Either way, a good game bird meal begins with proper field care.

In the Field

Game birds should be cooled down gradually. If the weather is warm, don't leave birds in the sun or in a hot game bag for long periods. Put them in a cool location and, if at all possible, let air circulate around them. It's usually best to field dress the birds after the day's hunt. Then hang, refrigerate, or freeze them before picking or skinning. Yes, I do freeze game birds with the feathers on. I believe it prevents the birds from drying out or getting freezer burn. You can also skin the birds at the same time you gut them in the field, refrigerating or freezing them depending on your philosophy and travel plans.

Preparing Birds for Travel

Here's how I handle birds on a hunting trip. Each day after hunting, I gut the birds, leaving the feathers on. If it's cool I hang them. If it's warm I wrap each bird in newspaper and place it in a cooler with plastic ice packs at the bottom. The birds stay dry and the newspaper helps insulate the cooler.

When traveling by air, I take the cooler full of birds with me. If the birds have been hung, I wrap them in newspaper and place them in a cardboard box before shipping.

If I'm on an extended driving trip I keep the birds in a cooler for several days, then find a way to keep them frozen. Once home, I place each bird in a Ziploc bag and freeze it.

Preparing Birds for the Taxidermist

A taxidermist can preserve your wingshooting memories for years to come. It's important to find a taxidermist whose work is pleasing to your eye, as styles often differ. Ask around about taxidermists near home, or contact the local chamber of commerce or a sporting goods store if you want to find a taxidermist while on a long trip. Get some references or go see his work. The Internet is also a great resource. Simply go to one of the major search engines and type in what you're looking for. Select a few likely candidates, and request testimonials or pictures of his work.

Mature birds make the best mounts. Select a bird that isn't too damaged and blot any leaking fluids, although a bird that has some blood on it can be taken care of by a taxidermist. Smooth the feathers and let the bird cool down,

Vehicles in the Field

Most of my bird hunting takes place far off the main gravel roads, so I use a reliable vehicle that can traverse the backcountry without getting into difficulty. Sometimes this means driving on two-rut dirt roads, section-line roads, or even tractor lanes used only for planting and harvest. In walk-in and wildlife management areas   park in designated zones. I stick to the landowner's established roads and never create new trails. I do the same on public land, staying only on designated roads.

Most trucks and SUVs have four-wheel drive in high and low ranges. These are wonderful hunting vehicles, but just because your rig is the ideal hunting buggy around home doesn't mean it can go anywhere. Tires are one important consideration. Some are better for sandy soil, other for "gumbo" or rocky terrain.

Driving down into a coulee may seem easy enough, but a sudden rain or snowstorm could make getting back out difficult to impossible. A rainstorm a day before a hunting trip should put you on guard. Different kinds of soil absorb and hold water differently. After a hard rain, gumbo may quickly develop on previously hard-packed roads, while sandy terrain often has deep ruts that can be difficult to clear.

Jacks, come-along, winches, and other accessories can sometimes get you out of a backcountry predicament when help is many miles away. If do carry such equipment, think of it only in terms of an unforeseen emergency, not as an excuse to take unnecessary chances. I always have a good shovel in my vehicle, and these days, having a cell phone along isn't a bad idea, either. One last word about hunting off the beaten path: Make sure you have an extra set of keys for your hunting partner. I also like to duct-tape an extra key to the undercarriage of hunting rig, so I never have to worry about being locked out or losing a key.

then wrap it in something soft. A paper towel or newspaper works fine. Just make sure the feathers aren't ruffled.

After the day's hunt, put the bird in a Ziploc bag and place it in a cooler or freeze it. Once frozen, the bird can last several months before being worked on. If you need to ship the bird, call your taxidermist for instructions.

Directory for Information Gathering

State Fish and Game Departments

Alabama Division of Game & Fish
64 N Union Street
Montgomery, AL 36130
334-242-3469
www.denr.state.al.us/agfd

Alaska Department of Fish & Game
P.O. Box 25526
Juneau, AK 99802
907-465-4100
www.state.ak.us/adfg

Arizona Game & Fish Department
2221 W. Greenway Road
Phoenix, AZ 85023
602-942-3000
www.state.azgfd.com

Arkansas Game & Fish Commission
2 Natural Resources Drive
Little Rock, AR 72205
501-223-6300
www.agfc.com

California Department of Fish & Game
1416 9th Street
Sacramento, CA 95814
916-653-7664
www.dfg.ca.gov

Colorado Division of Wildlife
6060 Broadway
Denver, CO 80216
303-29701192
www.wildlife.state.co.us

Connecticut Department of Environmental
Protection
79 Elm Street
Hartford, CT 06106
860-424-3011
www.dep.state.ct.us

Delaware Division of Fish & Wildlife
89 Kings Highway
Dover, DE 19901
302-739-5297
www.dnrec.state.de.us

Florida Fish & Wildlife Cons. Commission
620 S Meridian Street
Tallahassee, FL 32399
850-922-4330
www.floridacoserservation.org

Georgia Wildlife Resources Division
2111 US 278 SE
Social Circle, GA 30025
770-918-6416
www.georgiawildlife.com

Idaho Fish & Game Department
P.O. Box 25
600 S Walnut Street
Boise, ID 83707
208-334-3700
ww.state.id.us/fishgame

Illinois Department of Natural Resources
1 Natural Resources Way
Springfield, IL 62702
217-782-6424
www.dnr.state.il.us

Indiana Division of Fish & Game
402 W. Washington Street
Room W 273
Indianapolis, IN 46204
317-232-4080
www.wildlife.in.gov

Iowa Department of Natural Resources
502 E. 9th
Wallace State Office Bldg.
Des Moines, IA 50319
515-281-5918
www.state.ia.us/dnr

Kansas Department of Wildlife & Parks
512 SE 25th Avenue
Pratt, KS 67124
316-672-5911
www.kdwp.state.ks.us

Kentucky Department of Fish & Wildlife
1 Game Farm Road
Frankfort, KY 40601
1-800-858-1549
www.kdfwr.state.ky.us

Maine Dept. of Inland Fisheries & Wildlife
41 State House Station
284 State Street
Augusta, ME 04333
207-287-8000
www.state.me.us/ifw

Maryland Dept. of Natural Resources
580 Taylor Avenue
Wildlife & Heritage Division
Annapolis, MD 21401
410-260-8540
www.dnr.state.md.us

Massachusetts Dept. of Fish & Wildlife
251 Causeway Street
Suite 400
Boston, MA 02114
617-626-1590
www.state.ma.us/dfwele

Michigan Department of Natural Res.
P.O. Box 30444
Wildlife Division
Lansing, MI 48909
517-373-1263
www.dnr.state.mi.us

Minnesota Department of Natural Res.
500 Lafayette Road N
St. Paul, MN 55155
651-296-6157
www.dnr.state.mn.us

Mississippi Department of Wildlife,
Fisheries & Parks
1505 Eastover Drive
Jackson, MS 39211
601-432-2400
www.mdwfp.com

Missouri Department of Conservation
2901 W. Truman Boulevard
P.O. Box 180
Jefferson City, MO 65109
573-751-4115
www.conservation.state.mo.us

Montana Dept. of Fish, Wildlife & Parks
1420 E. 6th Avenue
Helena, MT 59620
406-444-2950
www.fwp.state.mt.us

Nebraska Game & Parks Commission
2200 N 33rd Street
Lincoln, NE 68503
402-471-0641
www.ngpc.state.ne.us

Nevada Division of Wildlife
1100 Valley Road
Reno, NV 89512
775-688-1500
www.nevadadivisionofwildlife.org

New Hampshire Fish & Game
Department
Public Affairs Division
2 Hazen Drive
Concord, NH 03301
603-271-2461
www.wildlife.state.nh.us

New Jersey Division of Fish & Wildlife
P.O. Box 400
Trenton, NJ 08625
609-292-2965
www.state.nj.us/dep/fgw

New Mexico Game & Fish Department
P.O. Box 25112
Santa Fe, NM 87504
505-827-7911
www.gmfsh.state.nm.us

New York Department of Environmental
Conservation
625 Broadway
Albany, NY 12233
518-402-8845
www.dec.state.ny.us

North Carolina Wildlife Resources
Commission
1722 Mail Service Center
Division of Wildlife Management
Raleigh, NC 27699
919-733-7291
www.ncwildlife.org

North Dakota State Game & Fish Dept.
100 N Bismark Expressway
Bismark, ND 58501
701-328-6300
www.state.nd.us/gnf

Ohio Division of Wildlife
1840 Belcher Drive
Columbus, OH 43224
614-265-6300
www.dnr.state.oh.us/wildlife

Oklahoma Dept. of Wildlife Conservation
P.O. Box 53465
Wildlife Division
Oklahoma City, OK 73152
406-521-3851
ww.wildlifedepartment.com

Oregon Department of Fish & Game
P.O. Box 59
2501 SW First Avenue
Portland, OR 97207
503-872-5268
www.dfwstate.or.us

Pennsylvania Game Commission
2001 Elmerton Avenue
Harrisburg, PA 17110
717-784-250
www.pgc.state.pa.us

Rhode Island Division of Fish & Game
4808 Tower Hill Road
Wakefield, RI 02879
401-789-3094
www.state.ri.us/ dem

South Carolina Department of Natural
Resources
Rembert C Dennis Building
P.O. Box 167
Game and Fish Department
Columbia, SC 29202
803-734-3888

South Dakota Game, Fish & Parks
523 E. Capitol Avenue
Pierre, SD 57501
605-773-3485
www.state.sd.us/gfp

Tennessee Wildlife Resources Agency
Ellington Agricultural Center
P.O. Box 40747
Nashville, TN 37204
615-781-6610
www.state.tn/twra

Texas Parks & Wildlife Department
4200 Smith School Road
Austin, TX 78744
1-800-792-1112
www.tpwd.state.tx.us

Utah Department of Natural Resources
1594 W North Temple
Division of Wildlife Resources
Salt Lake City, UT 84114
801-538-4700
www.wildlife.utah.gov

Vermont Fish & Wildlife Department
103 S Main Street
10 S. Building
Waterbury, VT 05671
802-241-3700
www.anr.state.vt.us

Virginia Department of Game & Inland
Fisheries
4010 W Broad Street
Richmond, VA 23230
804-367-1000
www.dgif.state.va.us

Washington Department of Fish &
Wildlife
600 Capitol Way N.
Olympia, WA 98501
360-902-2200
www.wa.gov/wdfw

West Virginia Division of Natural Res.
1900 Kanawha Boulevard E.
State Capital Complex Bldg. 3
Charleston, WV 25305
304-558-2758
www.dnr.state.wv.us

Wisconsin Department of Natural Res.
191 S. Webster Street
Madison, WI 53707
608-266-2621
www.dnr.state.wi.us

Wyoming Game & Fish Department
5400 Bishop Boulevard
Cheyenne, WY 82006
307-777-4600
www.gf.state.wy.us

Provincial Fish and Game Departments

Alberta Fisheries & Wildlife Management
Division
Main Floor South Tower
Petroleum Plaza
9915 108th Street
Edmonton, AB T5K 2G8
780-944-0313
www.gov.ab.ca/srd

British Columbia Ministry of the
Environment, Lands & Parks
P.O. Box 9360 Wildlife Branch
Stn. Provincial Gov.
Victoria, BC V8W 9M2
250-397-9422
www.gov.bc.ca/wlap

Manitoba Department of Natural
Resources
200 Salteaux Cresc
Winnipeg, MB R3J 3W3
1-800-214-6495
www.gov.mb.ca/natres

New Brunswick Department of Natural
Resources
Fish & Wildlife Branch
P.O. Box 6000
Fredricton, NB E3B 5H1
506-453-3826
www.nbgov.nb.ca

Newfoundland Department of Forest
Resources & Agrifoods
Wildlife Division, Bldg. 810, Pleasantville
P.O. Box 8700
St John's, NF A1B 4J6
709-729-2630
www.gov.nf.ca/forest

Northwest Territories Resources, Wildlife
& Economic Development
5th Floor, Scotia Building
600, 5102-50th Avenue
Yellowknife, NT X1A 3S8
867-920-6401
www.wildlife.rwed.gov.nt.ca

Nova Scotia Department of Natural
Resources
P.O. Box 698
Halifax, NS B3J 2T9
902-424-5935
www.gov.ns.ca/natr

Ontario Natural Resources Information
Center
P.O. Box 7000
300 Water Street, 1st Floor
Peterborough, ON K9J 8M5
705-755-2000
www.mnr.gov.on.ca

Prince Edward Island Department of
Technology & Environment
Fish & Wildlife Division
P.O. Box 2000
11 Kent Street
Charlettetown, PE C1A 7N8
902-368-5830
www.gov.pe.ca

Quebec Department of Recreation
Fish & Wildlife Division
150 Rene Levesque E., 8th Floor
Quebec City, PQ G1R 4Y1
418-643-2057

Saskatchewan Environment Resource
Management
Fish & Wildlife Branch, Room 436
3211 Albert Street
Regina, SK S4S 5W6
306-787-2314
www.seim.gov.sk.ca

Yukon Renewable Resources
Fish & Wildlife Branch
P.O. Box 2703
Whitehorse, YK Y1A 2C6
867-667-5811
www.gov.yk.ca

Map Sources

Commercial Maps:

DeLorme Mapping Company
Two DeLorme Drive
P.O. Box 298
Yarmouth, ME 04096
1-800-452-5931 or 207-865-417
www.delorme.com
The DeLorme Atlas & Gazetteer, all fifty
states: www delorme.com

Benchmark Maps
Map Link
30 South La Patera Lane, Unit 5
Goleta, CA 93117
805-692-6777
www.maplink.com
Benchmark Maps, available for western
states: www.benchmark map.com

Public Map Sources:

BLM Maps

U.S. Bureau of Land Management
Office of Public Affairs
1849 C Street Room406-LS
Washington, DC 20240
202-452-5125
For regional offices, visit: www.blm.gov

Forest Service Maps

Washington Office
Sydney R. Yates Building
201 14th Street SW
Washington DC 20024
202-205-8333
    (Mailing Address)
    P.O. Box 96090
    Washington, DC 20090-6090
For regional offices, visit: www.fs fed.us

USGS Maps

U.S. Geological Survey
Information Services
P.O. Box 25286
Denver, CO 80225
888-ASK-USGS
inforservices@usgs.gov

Maps, all states: www.50state.com

Internet Sites

State Fish and Wildlife Agencies, all states: www.dfw.state.or.us/ODFWhtml/MiscFiles/StateLink2.html

U.S. Fish & Wildlife Service: ww.fws.gov Region Offices: www.dfw.state.com

Bureau of Land Management: www.blm.gov

U.S. Army Corps of Engineers: Search for hunting at www.usace.army.mil

Forest Service, national forests and grasslands: www.fs fed.us/recreation

U.S. Geological Survey: www.usgs.gov

State information about destinations & misc. websites

www.tourstates.com

Specific state tourism information: www.2chambers.com

National directory for state and town facilities: www.travel.com

Traveling information for dogs: www.dogpile.com

Pet-friendly accommodations: www.petswelcome.com or www.peton-thego.com

Vet locations: www.veterinariansdirectory.com or www.americanveterinariansdirectory.com

Camping: www.CampUSA.com or www.camping.usa.com or www.the.campground.network.com